AWAKEN the GENIUS IN YOUR CHILD

Through
Positive Attitude Training

BY
NICOLA M. TAURASO, M.D., F.A.A.P., F.R.S.H.
Founder and Director
The GOTACH Center for Health
Frederick, Maryland

and

REV. L. RICHARD BATZLER, Ph.D.
Pastor, Faith-Mt. Pleasant United Church of Christ
Frederick, Maryland

Hidden Valley Press
7051 Poole Jones Road
Frederick, Maryland 21701

**Awaken The Genius In Your Child
Through Positive Attitude Training**

Copyright © 1981 Nicola M. Tauraso

All rights reserved, including the right to reproduce this
book or portions thereof in any form, except for the inclusion
of brief quotations in a review.

All inquiries should be addressed to:
        Hidden Valley Press
        7051 Poole Jones Road
        Frederick, Maryland 21701

First Printing, 1981

Printed in U.S.A.

Library of Congress Catalog Number: 81-80516

ISBN: 0-935710-01-9

DEDICATION

To George Ann Mudge for her undaunting faith, encouragement, and inspiration to pursue this work; to my sister Phyllis: thanks for opening the door; to my children (Angela Michele, Andrea, and Michael Angelo) for all they taught me about psychosocial motivations of children, and to all those children and young adults who are helped by this book.

ABOUT GENIUS

Genius is one of the most beautiful and significant words in our language. The word genius is derived from the Latin and French meaning "to beget, to give birth to." Other definitions describe genius as: animating spirit, special mental endowment, transcendental ability, extraordinary intelligence, outstanding gift for specialized activity, and extraordinary power of invention or organization of any kind.

Genius can be appropriately redefined as being that aspect of an individual's state of being which represents an ongoing desire to pursue and express perfection in any area.

These definitions speak of a mental and spiritual quality and power within persons that enable, ennoble, and enhance human life. Since it is the spirit which represents the energy-life-force within the individual, the potential of expression of genius is almost limitless. Freeing one from confining ways and developing and maintaining positive attitudes about one's true capabilities and self-worth is a prerequisite before genius can be realized.

We firmly believe that all persons have genius within, and that a major goal in life is to awaken that genius so that life here and now will be more beautiful, abundant, and meaningful. It is this belief and this goal that have motivated the writing of this book.

Nicola M. Tauraso, M.D.
L. Richard Batzler, Ph.D.

TABLE OF CONTENTS

DEDICATION   III

ACKNOWLEDGEMENTS   IX

PREFACE   XIII

FOREWORD   XV

1. THE NEED FOR POSITIVE ATTITUDE TRAINING IN CHILDREN   1
   What is positive attitude training (PAT)? Goals. Why do children need it? How can they be trained? When and where should PAT be done? Summary. The Garden of Life. Planting seeds.

2. CHILDREN'S RELATIONSHIPS WITH SELF AND OTHERS   11
   Self. Belief creates reality. Parents. Siblings. Friends and peers. Teachers and other authority figures. Subordinates. Identity within the garden.

3. ATTITUDES ABOUT GOD 27
Introduction. Significance of positive attitudes about God. Some specific exercises for developing positive attitudes about God. The Source of energy.

4. MENTAL TRAINING: THE KEY TO PAT 39
General aspects. The brain and the mind: are they the same? How the mind functions. The conscious and subconscious minds. Exciting information from mind/brain research: right vs. left brain. Mental activities related to brain waves and states of consciousness. The three keys to mind power. Obstacles to growth. The four keys of self-development and self-realization: self-responsibility, self-awareness, self-control, and self-discipline. Superlearning. Summary. The garden architect.

5. POSITIVE ATTITUDE TRAINING (PAT) TECHNIQUES 65
Introduction. Affirmation: to develop positive belief factor; Belief Affirmations; Plans for Living: for developing self-responsibility; for increasing self-awareness; for developing self-control; for developing self-discipline. Meditation: Technique. Guided imagery: Technique. Summary. The garden worker.

6. THE HOME ENVIRONMENT 81
Conception to birth. The first year. Ages one to five. Six to eleven. Twelve to seventeen. Eighteen to twenty. Postscript. The winter-early spring garden environment.

TABLE OF CONTENTS

7. **THE SCHOOL ENVIRONMENT AND STUDY HABITS**   97
   Introduction. Kindergarten. First to sixth grade. Seventh to ninth grade. Tenth to twelfth grade. Summary. The late spring environment.

8. **THE PLAY ENVIRONMENT**   107
   Introduction. Harmful games adults play with children. Games children play can tell you something. Fantasies. Dreams. Movies and TV. How to transform games and play into useful realities. Play in the garden.

9. **EFFECTS OF MEDICINE AND OTHER DRUGS ON ATTITUDE**   121
   General aspects. Physical damage caused by psychotropic drugs: the suppression of natural defense and treatment mechanisms; the suppression of physical strength. Addiction. Suppression of mental and natural creative abilities. The hyperactive child. Conclusion. How to control the weeds.

10. **EFFECTS OF DIET**   135
    Introduction. Effects of diet on mental and emotional health. Effects on concentration, learning, and memory. Toxic foods. How allergy affects various dis-ease conditions and behavior in children. The No-No list of foods. Case histories. Schedule for meals. Fasting. Conclusion. Nutrients in the garden.

TABLE OF CONTENTS

11. EFFECT OF EXERCISE ON MENTAL
    ATTITUDES 167
    Introduction. General comments about metabolism. Aerobic vs. anaerobic exercise. Effect of exercise on physical, mental, emotional, and spiritual health. School exercise programs. Conclusion. Plants exercise too.

12. SPIRITUAL TRAINING 175
    Introduction. Basic factors in spiritual training. A garden reflects the spirit of the master gardener.

13. RESPONSIBILITY OF PARENTS 187
    Introduction. General aspects. Preparation for life outside the home. Teaching goal setting. Authority support. Application of a PAT program. The garden teachers.

14. RESPONSIBILITY OF TEACHERS
    AND SCHOOL SYSTEM 199
    Introduction. General Aspects. Learning disabilities: poor concentration; poor memory; dyslexia; hyperactivity. Prevention and treatment of learning disabilities. Development of self-esteem. Peer pressure. Getting along with others. Early vs. late onset of school. Summary. The garden advisers.

15. THE CHALLENGE OF RAISING CHILDREN
    TO HAVE POSITIVE ATTITUDES 215
    Introduction. The philosophy. Application of philosophy. Conclusion. The garden at harvest.

SUGGESTED READINGS 227

ACKNOWLEDGEMENTS

There are numerous individuals who contributed, both knowingly and unknowingly, to this work. The children with whom we have worked through the years provided us with valuable data and experience.

There are many parents who are sensitive to their children's needs to the degree that they are searching beyond what is customarily available as a resource for creative ways to raise and stimulate their children. Many of these parents have encouraged us and continue to do so in our work.

The most special gratitude and thanks to George Ann Mudge who shares the dedication of this book with my children. Her undaunting faith, patience, support, and encouragement were everpresent during all phases of our work with children and the actual writing of this book. She has always believed that our work with children should be paramount and we agree on this.

It was George Ann who interceded in my behalf and secured the mountain cabin of Jean Higgins, where I spent time in seclusion, meditating, generating ideas, and writing the major portion of the initial manuscript. The mountains overlooking the Blair Valley in northwestern Maryland were extremely conducive to our special creation. My thanks to Jean for allowing me to use her home and providing this very special atmosphere. I acknowledge the inspiration and help of Rev. L. Richard Batzler, Ph.D., who is much more than just a collaborator in this work. He is both a friend and spiritual brother. As spiritual advisor to our Center, he shares his unique gift of spiritual insight. His contributions of Chapters 3 (Attitudes about God) and 12 (Spiritual Training) reflect both his competency and commitment and sensitivity to the Word. In addition, his advice during all aspects of preparing the manuscript and his editorial assistance helped considerably in refining this work.

A very particular thanks to Filomena C. Morton, my sister, for her fearless and painstaking efforts in critically reviewing the manuscript. Fil always comes through when the need arises.

We acknowledge the interest Dudley Lyons took in our work. Dudley and his beautiful and charming wife, Volina, sent their two lovely children, Tory and Greg, to our 1980 camp. It was Dudley who presented a copy of the manuscript to Dr. Arthur Caliandro (minister at the Marble Collegiate Church, New York City) who, recognizing the importance of our work, in turn, asked the Reverend Doctor Norman Vincent Peale to review it. Our deepest gratitude to Dudley, Art and Norman Vincent Peale for their efforts of encouragement and inspiration, and to Dr. Peale for writing the Preface.

We are grateful to Eileen Dunnell, the latest member of The GOTACH Center for Health team, for her valuable editorial help and for proofreading

ACKNOWLEDGEMENTS

the final manuscript and galleys. Thanks also to Fay W. Joy for her preparation and donation of the artwork for Figures 4-1 and 8-1.

We are indebted to the staffs of Hidden Valley Press and Hagerstown Bookbinding and Printing for their help, and especially for their willingness and availability to work closely during all stages of transforming the manuscript into the final book. We especially single out Perk Hull of HBP for his artistic creation of the concept for the book cover.

We acknowledge the fine artistry of Mary C. Bausman in the Garden of Life drawings.

We are also taking this opportunity to thank all those who purchase a copy of this book, for they should know that **all** the proceeds derived from sales are being donated to The GOTACH Center for Health for building a residential/camp facility to be dedicated to and used by children to teach and help them *awaken* their *genius.*

Nicola M. Tauraso

PREFACE

Dr. Tauraso and Rev. Batzler have written a superb book, one I wish had been on my desk when I was the father of young children. This book is filled with practical wisdom on how to recognize the great potential that lies within the personality of every child. Most parents believe there is something special deep inside their children and want to see it develop, but they don't know how it can be released.

All too often being a parent becomes considerable frustration and disappointment. Any who read this book and follow the profound truths which are stated in terms that are clear, concise and easy to understand cannot help but succeed in raising their children into healthy and successful adults. In addition, they will enjoy their task as parents.

That the book emphasizes positive attitudes is no surprise to me, for I know what a tremendous difference a positive attitude can make. The replacement of a negative approach with a positive one completely changes one's life. The child thus raised becomes the beneficiary of good mental conditioning. A positive attitude is like a catalytic agent in releasing the tremendous hidden powers and resources of a personality.

Although this book is written for parents who are trying to do a more effective job in raising their children, I think the scientific and spiritual principles spelled out so well by Dr. Tauraso and Rev. Batzler will help anyone, whether he is a parent or not. The thoughts on meditation, getting rid of bad habits, taking care of life by proper diet and exercise, and developing self discipline will help awaken the genius in any adult.

Norman Vincent Peale

FOREWORD

Learning to cope with the everyday challenges of life has become the major concern of almost every individual. Many are recognizing this and are seeking help and assistance from others in their search for solutions. Many are recognizing how difficult it is to turn their lives around from a negative deteriorating condition to a positive uplifting experience.

Habits are difficult to break and change. This is not only true for those easily recognizable habits of smoking and overeating, but also true for the bad habits of living, lack of concentration, poor memory, and failure. What is the best way of controlling these bad habits? It is by not developing them in the first place, by having developed good habits during youth.

This book is an attempt to describe some of the problems that begin to develop in children and young adults which tend to interfere with positive psychosocial development, and to present ways by which children can learn to develop their natural abilities and talents for their own personal growth.

The greatest advances in the field of health have not been in therapy of dis-ease states. They have been in prevention. One needs only to think of the millions of lives saved from dis-eases, such as the plague, dysentery illnesses (e.g., typhoid fever, cholera), yellow fever, typhus, diphtheria, whooping cough, tetanus, and more recently, polio, measles, and smallpox, to name only a few. All of these dis-eases have been successfully eradicated or controlled by preventive measures.

We now realize that the key to controlling the physical health scourges of modern man (e.g., heart disease and cancer) is not in therapy: medications and cardiac by-pass surgery for the cardiac; surgery, radio- and chemo-therapy for the cancer patient. The key lies in prevention.

Why not consider the same might be true for mental and psychological disturbances which not only interfere with our actualizing our full potential, but in many individuals result in their own destruction? Bad habits are difficult to break and change, but **good** habits are just as deeply ingrained and difficult to change. Learning good habits early in life is a **must** if we wish to be creative, productive, successful, and happy.

This book emerged both as a result of our experiences in, and a need for some form of an instruction manual for, our T-H-E-M-E Positive Attitude Training Camps for Children and Young Adults. It is written primarily for parents upon whom the responsibility rests of rearing and guiding their children to their full potential, and it is for those children mature enough to appreciate that they **can** control their destiny. This book is also useful for teachers, ministers, physicians, and others who interact with children during their growth and development years.

FOREWORD

A beautiful and fascinating element of nature is that the *human is endowed with fantastic capabilities for self-development.* (GOTACH Biological Law #1). We have been given power over ourselves. If we are willing to assume **total** self-responsibility, develop greater and greater self-awareness, learn self-control through self-discipline, there is almost no limit to what we can achieve. **Belief creates reality.** We hope that through this book parents will begin to help *awaken the genius* within their children and to help them develop strong psyches so that they may learn to deal with life creatively.

It is our hope that readers exchange their concerns, ideas, and experiences with us so that we can all learn how to develop our most important resource — children.

Nicola M. Tauraso, M.D.
L. Richard Batzler, Ph.D.

CHAPTER 1

THE NEED FOR POSITIVE ATTITUDE TRAINING IN CHILDREN

What is positive attitude training (PAT)?

PAT is a system by which an individual learns how to develop positive, constructive, uplifting and creative attitudes toward **all** phases of life's experiences.

This is not new. It is essentially the basis of the monumental works of such giants as Norman Vincent Peale and of all training systems and courses from Dale Carnegie, Silva Mind Control, and Earl Nightingale to some of the more recently developed programs of self-improvement. The many books, cassette tapes and courses on this subject have helped many individuals realize success, prosperity, better health, and more fulfilling and happy lives.

However, many who have taken these programs have not achieved what they had hoped for. Although this does not detract from the usefulness of these programs, it does make you ask the question: why the failures?

Our purpose here is not to analyze the answer to this question, other than to state the reasons may vary anywhere from lack of successful communication between the instructor and the student, lack of full appreciation by the individual of how deep seated his or her challenges are, and of the energy and work required to change, to lack of motivation and desire to alter one's pattern of living.

We declare that the chief reason for many individuals failing to alter their course in life is that habits are difficult to break. *Habits are programmed patterns of behavior deeply rooted in our subconscious mind* which function at an energy state **higher** than the conscious mind we try to use to change habits. Although changing habits is difficult, it is not impossible.

The GOTACH Center is an holistic health facility devoted to teaching individuals how to assume responsibility over their lives, especially in health matters, how to develop an ever increasing self-awareness of the meaning of their consciousness, and how to learn self-control through self-discipline. We are deeply committed to teaching wellness and preventive medicine. An important aspect of this total philosophy is habit control through prevention.

PAT of children and young adults is a learning experience whereby good habits of behavior are developed through practice, in the same natural way that occurs in the development of bad habits.

The ideas and techniques described in this book are results of our experiences with children in our T-H-E-M-E Positive Attitude Training Summer Camps for Children and Young Adults. The meaning of the acronym T-H-E-M-E (Total Holistic Enrichment through Meditative Enlightenment) will become evident as the book progresses. Individuals wishing to know more about these camps can write The GOTACH Center, 7051 Poole Jones Road, Frederick, Maryland 21701 for more information.

Goals

Children and young adults undergoing PAT learn how to:
— Develop their natural abilities and talents for their own personal growth
— Concentrate, improve memory, and succeed in school; improve study habits and learn to communicate with self and others
— Develop self-motivation, self-esteem, self-control, and self-discipline at home, at school, and with friends
— Be creative and productive in their personal, educational, and social lives
— Expand awareness and inspire positive attitudes
— Actualize their potential and develop leadership qualities during their early years.

Why do children need it?

If children and young adults were to develop good habits of behavior, there would be little need to expend so much energy just to *keep their heads above the water* and survive later in life when they wish to participate in much more constructive events.

Table 1-1 lists some of the common problems facing adults today. The list is by no means all-inclusive. All of these conditions in one way or another are unwanted habits learned early in life as children. Wouldn't it be better to learn a good habit corresponding to each of these negative situations?

Table 1-1
Common Problems Facing Adults Today

habit control:
  smoking, overeating, gambling
stress and tension-related illnesses
  headaches, hypertension, pain
difficulty sleeping
poor general health
lack of vitality
poor concentration and memory
inability to solve problems and make decisions
lack of creativity
poor self-image
failure in personal and vocational endeavors

Let us consider some of the medical conditions common among our modern children: hyperactivity, bedwetting, high blood pressure, headaches, asthma, ulcers, irritable bowel syndrome, constipation, to name a few. Additionally, there are many children experiencing disciplinary problems, tension and stress, poor concentration and study habits, poor self-image, negative attitudes, and other related conditions which tend to interfere with positive psychosocial development. These conditions and many others become programmed negative habits which either continue or are transformed to other negative experiences in the adult. If the philosophy of prevention, by instilling good habits, were to be applied in childhood, it would allow many to achieve a more meaningful life longer. PAT helps to achieve this goal.

PAT can and does help all children, including those with no particular negative challenges, to be more creative and become decision makers, to improve concentration, memory and problem solving, and to control habits which tend to decrease their ability to achieve.

The overall most important goal of PAT is **to teach individuals to develop their innate abilities to reach full potential,** that is, *to awaken their genius.*

How can they be trained?

The purpose of this book is to answer this question by describing ways of teaching children how to use their minds for constructive living.

PAT does not come as a panacea pill that you take once and the desired effect occurs permanently. PAT has to be an ongoing experience of increasing self-awareness, self-control, and self-discipline to be effective.

We shall see that PAT begins at conception and should be reinforced throughout life. It may be work at first, but later as good habits are developed and reinforced it **does** become easier and easier to experience the good life.

Parents need to appreciate the tremendous influence they have as example givers to children, even to those who may appear to demonstrate rebellious behavior. Parents need to become more involved in demanding that schools and teachers cooperate in their roles as **temporary** custodians of their children. Parents can take a more active role and make a more sustained effort in performing the mental exercises which are required to train the child's mind to be more useful and productive.

A major challenge for teachers, who automatically inherit *pre-programmed* students, is to teach children to be constructive rather than negative thinkers. Techniques designed to teach individuals increasing mental awareness are now beginning to be implemented as a part of the curriculum in some schools in addition to standard age-proven subjects of *reading, 'riting, and 'rithmetic.*
More specific PAT techniques are described as the book progresses.

When and where should PAT be done?

We are proposing PAT for children because it is more effective to teach individuals at a time when they are most receptive to new learning experiences rather than later in life when their minds are relatively closed to new ideas. There is an old saying, "You can't teach an old dog new tricks." It is my contention (which I realize has yet to be proven) that animals function primarily at a level akin to the subconscious level of humans. Just as animals are difficult to train or retrain when they get older, so humans experience difficulty changing subconscious habits later in life.

Children would benefit greatly by using PAT as an ongoing process. At early preschool age, it is primarily the responsibility of both parents. Unfortunately, negative input by well-meaning grandparents and relatives often thwarts the best intentions of parents.

Later during the school years, it becomes the joint effort of parents and teachers, with parents **always** in the driver's seat.

Parents can send their children to participate in programs (e.g., seminars, camps, schools) designed to teach PAT. A good program will orient parents as to what they can do to reinforce what their child has already learned. Both parents and teachers can learn PAT so that they can be more effective in teaching their children.

Summary

Much of our behavior as adults results from programmed habits originating in childhood. Whereas good habits produce meaningful, rewarding experiences, bad habits cause negative, self-destructive tendencies. Because habits are deep-seated subconscious patterns of behavior, they are difficult to break and change later in life. For this reason it becomes important to practice prevention of bad habits and to develop and maintain good mental habits early in life. PAT is a system of developing positive, constructive, and uplifting mental attitudes about all phases of life's experiences. It is primarily the parents' responsibility to institute this training and to insure its continued reinforcement until young adults are mature enough to continue the process themselves. The results are well worth the effort.

THE GARDEN OF LIFE

Planting seeds

Life can be viewed as a garden. Any person planting a vegetable or flower garden in the backyard knows that, before we can reap any meaningful harvest, we must first plant the seeds. The kind of harvest will depend upon the species and the quality of the seed. Wheat seeds produce wheat plants; tomato seeds, tomato plants; squash seeds, squash plants; weed and thistle seeds, weeds and thistles. Also, the earlier seeds are planted, the longer and more productive the season.

Thoughts, ideas and attitudes are the seeds of life. The quality of the thoughts and attitudes is determinative of a quality of life. Positive thoughts are the good seeds; negative thoughts are the weeds and thistles. If a mixture of good and bad thought seeds are planted, life becomes a struggle between the good and bad, the positive and negative, for survival. Life then consists of an ongoing series of stressful events.

Also, the earlier these thoughts, ideas and attitudes are planted, the more secure and rooted they become. It is important to start early in the spring of life to plant the seeds of positive thoughts and attitudes so that the ongoing harvest bears good fruit in body, mind and spirit.

CHAPTER 2

CHILDREN'S RELATIONSHIPS WITH SELF AND OTHERS

Self

First and foremost in a child's development is relationship with self. During the very early days, weeks, and months after birth, one cannot chronologically separate developing relationships with others, especially parents, but for the sake of this discussion we will take that liberty. The infant is spatially distinct from, yet is **totally** dependent upon, others. This situation creates within the infant an early concern about his own identity and independence.

The infant is hungry and must depend upon another for food. The diaper gets wet and messy and someone else must again solve this problem. The infant wants something; another must supply his wishes. Have we ever asked the question: what is happening to this infant's developing self-esteem when he or she must depend upon someone else for fulfillment of every desire?

Ellen G. White, in her book *Child Guidance,* discusses the child's desire to rule the roost and dominate the household. We see this happening in many family situations and it can start as early as the day the infant comes home from the hospital after birth. It has been said that infants cannot be spoiled at this age. Don't kid yourself! It can happen at any age!

Is this infant's desire to rule the roost a way of minimizing dependency upon others and bolstering his own self-worth and esteem? One can entertain the possibility that it might be a causative factor. There is nothing wrong with an infant's desire to determine his own destiny; however, without knowledge and maturity, infants and children lack the ingredients necessary for correct decisions. So, *the ability to make decisions must await the corresponding degree of maturity.*

What can be done in the meantime? One important consideration when rearing children is to support their egos frequently. Whenever they seem to fail, attempt to instill the spirit of achievement — that with practice they can be satisfied with themselves. An accomplished figure-skating team does not achieve success in every maneuver after the first try. It may take many attempts after many errors to achieve success. As with steel which requires the correct amount of tempering to become a useful metal, so it is with an individual's ego which also requires trying, failing, and trying again to be tempered into strength.

Of special significance here, we suggest that the goal being supervised by the authority figure be an **attainable** one for the particular child's stage of physical and mental development, e.g., trying to teach an under-teen of average size to accomplish proficiency with a basketball net set up for adult regulation height would plant seeds of frustration rather than a sense of satisfaction. Let us rather make it *reachable,* then raise it gradually according to the child's sense of accomplishment.

Too many parents tend to overprotect children to the point that progress in the maturing process becomes indefinitely delayed. Preparing children for an independent life outside the confines of the home can be a challenging responsibility for parents. However, it would be well for us, as parents, to practice letting go and to allow children to express their state or stage of development.

When we assist children to develop self-esteem and self-worth, it becomes their legacy to be self-reliant and self-realized.

As children develop they may be given increasing responsibilities to demonstrate their capabilities. The judgement of when the time is correct to do this is what makes raising children the art that it is. No two children are alike, not even within the same family complex.

We have observed many children with shattered self-images and very low levels of self-esteem. An example of this situation might be a shy and withdrawn child, lacking the desire to interact with peers and adults other than parents. Or it may be manifested as the belligerent child who is going to show everyone else in the world what a powerful individual he is, but never quite actually realizing it himself. His inferiority complex is known to everyone but himself.

Belief creates reality

As we shall explain later on, it is the subconscious belief individuals have about themselves that is important. If children believe and see themselves as losers, then losers they are. If they see themselves as winners, then winners they are.

More often, what individuals think of themselves is hidden from their conscious reality. This is where increasing self-awareness becomes important to an individual's development. It is truly a satisfying feeling to start taking measures in knowing one's self, thereby opening the door to understanding others.

PAT can and has helped children develop positive self-images and bolster self-esteem. Additionally, it has helped others restore and repair shattered self-images.

Parents

The first authority figures a child encounters are parents, and children soon learn that these parents are like no other authority figures they will ever meet.

Parents can sometimes be most predictable and at other times most unpredictable. They can be both consistent and inconsistent. They can appear to the child as all-loving and, on occasion, most vengeful. What's a child to do? (The same views and interpretations can also be made by parents of their children!)

Most of the time parents are generally aware of the correct thing to do, but the implementation of it is often lost because of uncontrolled positive or negative emotions.

Even though children may try to control or thwart their parents' desires, they usually deeply admire their parents. When children observe flaws in their parents' personalities, they may either accept and develop similar flaws or they may begin to learn how to deal with fallen idols.

Children are constantly learning the software programming of their developing biocomputer by observing their parents' behavior. Children seem to learn best by example. How does a mother react when she burns the dinner, or spills tomato sauce on her brand-new dress, or crashes the family automobile, or is rejected on her fifth job interview? How does a father react when he smashes his finger with a hammer, or is turned down for a promotion he thinks he deserves and expected, or loses his job with no visible means of support near at hand?

Does the parent fall apart, cry, become sullen and depressed, lose all hope? Does the parent begin to express anger by lashing out at his spouse, children, and friends?

The children are observing and computing. The next time seeming tragedy besets the child, does he express anger, fall apart, cry, or get depressed? Does he begin to reflect the behavior exhibited by his parents when they were stressed?

Our responsibility as parents is clear: to be aware of our behavior, i.e., to teach by example. If we want our children to be positive and uplifting, then let us be so ourselves. If we want our children to see themselves as winners, let us see ourselves as winners also. But remember to exercise a degree of humility rather than using a forceful parental Ego to convey our intention. Children generally desire to be like their parents. So let us insure that **we like what they see in us!**

Of the four key factors influencing self-development described in Chapter 4, self-discipline is the power source necessary to achieve the rest. Children can be taught discipline by using both firmness and kindness. Let us try to remember the role our own self-discipline plays as the example our children might strive for. If we lack discipline in controlling the habit of overeating or eliminating the smoking habit in ourselves, we can expect that children will apply the same degree of discipline in their study habits or in sharing their toys with others!

Children will learn to deal with other authority figures as they deal with their parents. Will they develop fear or respect for authority? Will they learn to fear or respect their teachers, the next major authority figure in line? Will they fear or respect their God? Will they fear or respect themselves?

Siblings

The major psychosocial factor some children face with siblings is how to deal with competition: for position in family, love of parents, material possessions such as toys, etc. How they learn to handle this aspect of their development will affect their competitive relationships in school with their peers and later on in their adult life.

A child's self-image will not only be affected by, but will also influence, his relationships with siblings. Again the major responsibility for orchestrating this family symphony rests upon the parental directors. Become cognizant of the many creative games children tend to play with family members as they vie for position, influence, and authority in the family government.

Children can learn to share responsibilities consonant with their increasing age and maturity. In fact it is good for them to begin to realize the awesome responsibility of authority. This can be a maturing responsibility in itself. Often, children do not participate in sharing chores around the house because they do not do the jobs as well as the parents would like. Asking children to assume their load of the work encourages their growth and maturity. Interaction among siblings is prob-

RELATIONSHIPS WITH SELF AND OTHERS 17

ably the first major setting where children learn to handle relationships. Insist that each child takes a share of the workload around the house.

We have seen large families with exceptional parents and each child carrying his load and being happy with it. We have also observed families with one to three children creating discord because of seeming inequality of chore responsibilities, eventually resulting in either parent doing all the work.

Children do play games with their siblings and parents, perhaps because they observe parents playing games between themselves. Think about it. Raising children is serious business. It is like no other profession in the world. Since we are not allowed the luxury of learning child rearing on a disposable child-unit which automatically self-destructs at age 18, we must attempt to do it correctly the first time around!

Many children develop healthy positive interrelationships with their siblings and learn to generate their own unique psyche, self-image, self-esteem, gifts, talents, and genius. PAT instituted in the home is designed to promote a healthy family team as a group effort. There was once a common expression, unfortunately not heard much in recent years, "A family that prays together stays together." Group energy is more than arithmetically additive; it can grow exponentially as described in Chapter 4. Families that practice some form of PAT as a group will experience much more effective programmings than if it were done individually.

Friends and peers

The next experience children face is learning to deal with friends and peers. This event is noteworthy because it is the first venture to occur outside the home government. The child can begin to test and experiment with ways to run his own show, and if things don't work out, then it's "my word against theirs," and "my parents always believe me."

Wise parents are always aware that their children's experiences may not be what they appear to be at first glance, nor are they frequently what parents desire. Children as well as parents tend to play emotional games — consciously and unconsciously — and sad are the parents and children who succumb to this trap.

As parents, experience teaches us not to take sides in most inter-peer disturbances, as they often tend to be fleeting misadventures. There are times when a child may experience difficulty with a friend that is not his fault. As a parent, are you eager to jump in, adding more fuel to your child's possible self-pity and indignation? Or are you creative in seizing this opportunity to teach your child understanding, tolerance, and forgiveness toward a friend?

With every action, there is a corresponding reaction. We live in a world of energy and energy requires polar opposites: plus and minus, love and hate, tolerance and intolerance, harmony and conflict, peace and chaos, to name a few. How we balance these forces determines how and to what degree our consciousness develops.

Children learn how to develop peer relationships by observing their parents interact with their friends. If we wish our children to learn love, understanding, tolerance, and forgiveness toward others, let us be aware of our emphasis on these in dealing with our friends and peers.

Relationships with friends need not be competi-

RELATIONSHIPS WITH SELF AND OTHERS   19

tive. We are creative beings and creativity allows us the freedom to overcome petty competitiveness.

Develop an interest in your children's friends. Attempt to influence children to surround themselves with positive uplifting friends, because we are affected by the energies of those with whom we surround ourselves. Children seem to be easily influenced by their friends — peer pressure. If this takes hold, influence as a parent becomes secondary. Peer pressure is one of the strongest forces influencing the behavior of children, especially in their adolescent years. Prepare them (and yourself) for this eventuality.

PAT can help your children develop strong healthy habits which will not be easily affected by the potential negative influence of their peers. In fact, your children's positive attitudes can instill a strong healthy influence into the peer group.

Teachers and other authority figures

The first major authority figures children encounter outside the home are teachers. As with most authority figures, but especially true here, teachers serve another role as models children tend to emulate and perhaps idolize. Teachers are constantly being scrutinized by their pupils. They are being compared with parents in many ways and the psychological games children play on their parents, they tend to play on their teachers, especially the ones they become successful at.

Teachers assign work and grade the effort. Additionally, they sometimes function as judges of behavior, and they mete out the punishment. All of this authority of the teacher has to be accepted and dealt with. Teachers, in turn, are being judged and sentenced, at least in the deep subconscious psychological world of the child, the only true place these events have meaning.

Children need to learn to cope with this authority. Whether they accept or reject it, or try to negotiate with or maneuver around it, determines how successful their school lives will be over a span of from 12 to 16 or more years.

Authority should be firm, kind, fair, and consistent. When individuals learn to balance all four of these ingredients, they can feel comfortable as the authority figures for children committed to their care.

Children respect consistency and fairness. They relate to kindness and accept firmness. Children will learn these ingredients by observing the way authority figures act around them.

Do you as a teacher verbally downgrade unjustly another teacher or your principal? Do you criticize local or national governments, policemen, etc., without leaving children something with which to rebuild the authority superstructure within their own minds? During the 1960s, we experienced in our country a growing disregard of authority by youth. The consequence was that youth had nothing with which to replace it. We saw young adults driven to escape through drugs. Psychological confusion reigned. Many of those individuals have come back to work within the organized framework of society, whereas others have never recovered. Although today's youth are probably wiser than their 1960 counterparts, many are still as, or more, confused as their predecessors. Children learn confusion as they learn everything else, and they learn it from those in authority.

Today we are experiencing an epidemic of confusion among adults; remember, the same adults who were children in the 1960s! This book is not intended to be a treatise on human behavior. But on occasion we have to refer to the problems of adults to see what it is we must prevent in the child. Confused children usually grow up to be confused adults; weak children, weak adults; intolerant children, intolerant adults; and so it would appear to be with love and hate, fear and fearlessness, harmony and chaos, etc. How individuals balance these entities as children, so they will do as adults.

What should teachers do; how should they do it? The answer is simple but not simplicity: teach by example.

This rule also applies to other authority figures such as relatives, bosses and supervisors, government officials, etc.

I am not suggesting that children blindly follow **all** authority — far from it. There is an inner authority within everyone of us which is above that authority outside of our being and there is an Authority above all mental authority into which we are subconsciously tuned — God. Individuals do get confused when communication with this higher Authority is interrupted (Chapter 3).

PAT can help children discover this higher authority within themselves. They can learn how to balance the ingredients of their emotions. Teachers can use the singular opportunity they have to help children develop their full potential for expression. Together they can strive to the highest levels of consciousness of which man is capable.

Subordinates

The true test of what children learn about authority can be observed in how they deal with subordinates: younger siblings, children in lower grades, individuals on the job as they get to be teenagers and begin to work.

Life is a constantly evolving learning experience. One day we may be observing, the next day doing, and the day after that teaching.

Children are learning about themselves, developing their own unique psyches. They interact with all kinds of separate and distinct entities: parents, relatives, friends, teachers, etc. Eventually, they become authority figures to other individuals. The true measure of what individuals are can truly be reflected in how they deal with individuals under their charge.

First on the scene might be younger siblings. Does a child view this younger family member as a competitive threat or as someone to be loved and cherished? Do the parents neglect, consciously or subconsciously, the older child, giving preference to the newly arrived sibling? Does the parent ask older children to begin to assume more responsibility to keep in step with their growing position in the hierarchy of family government? Are parents extra careful at this time to insure that the threatened child is not devastated but learns how to deal with the advent of a newborn?

Next on the scene may be younger relatives and friends, another important event as the child reaches out from the protected home environment. Have we prepared our children by example? Have we been careful in how we deal with subordinates in our lives? I once saw a cartoon of a boss shaking his reprimanding finger at one of his employees, who went home and shook his finger at his wife, who shook her finger at her child. The last block in the cartoon was the picture of the child shaking his finger at the unfortunate dog.

RELATIONSHIPS WITH SELF AND OTHERS

The truth in the cartoon is that example is a great teacher.

What and how children learn at this level will be applied at the next higher level, possibly work-related, and then onward throughout their adult lives.

PAT can help children learn how to deal with themselves as authority figures. In our summer camps we mix all ages of children and young adults from ages five to 19. The younger children learn to respect the older ones, who in turn learn how to act as authority figures and leaders. Separating children by ages so that only those ages five to nine, or ten to 13, or 14 and older, interact only with each other creates an artificial life experience. Teenagers, when they leave the camp, have to deal with older and younger individuals. The same is true for everyone.

PAT in a camp or seminar setting should prepare an individual for real life situations and events. Conducting our programs with all age groups has enabled us to learn more about the psychodynamics of developing interpersonal relationships and to apply this knowledge in improving our PAT program for children and young adults.

Identity within the garden

One of the prerequisites for proper growth within the garden is the inner strength of the plant. Too many plants growing together may choke each other out so that none grow to useful maturity. Barely does a single plant overcome the stifling effects of the others. Thinning out of plants and pruning of trees provide an environment wherein the plant establishes an identity with self and others. The strength of each plant supports and bolsters the strength of the others.

The garden of life requires similar conditions for growth and development of each individual. Ideal conditions toward developing healthy attitudes about self and others lead toward fruitful living.

CHAPTER 3

ATTITUDES ABOUT GOD

Introduction

An holistic approach to life always involves the recognition of the reality of the spiritual nature of persons and the value of nurturing the spirit. Any educational or philosophical system or any family training that does not include spirit as a central fact of man's existence is incomplete.

Attitudes about God constitute a significant force in awakening the genius and fostering wholeness in children. This fact is not readily recognized by many parents, who themselves often do not seek to understand or experience God in their lives. Such parents, when children question them about God, either change the subject or lightly dismiss the question and the child.

Today the lives of parents and children are usually so full of activities, schedules and plans dealing with persons, places, things and organizations, that spiritual realities are virtually non-existent for them. Pressures from the materialistic world tend to preclude serious consideration of that which is non-material. Sundays, traditionally a time of study and worship of God, is for so many now a day of excursions to the woods, shore, or shopping malls, mowing lawns, yard sales, majorette practice or other secular work or pleasure.

Traditional ways of teaching and learning about God now seem inadequate, not because these ways are wrong, but because they often don't speak to children or adults where they are in their psychosocial environment. God simply doesn't seem to fit in anywhere with their mental or emotional desires or needs or with the scientific and technical consciousness and phenomena which are experienced each day in some way.

Significance of positive attitudes about God

The recognition of these factors that hinder positive attitudes about God is an important first step in dealing with the challenge of God-realization in our lives. A second step is that of affirming the significance of the spiritual in our total life and then finding ways to activate this affirmation so that new awarenesses and sensitivities can emerge.

There are many forces operating in our beliefs and attitudes about God. Some of these forces are evident, others are more subtle and hidden. Generally, positive attitudes about God help to give balance (God as gyroscope) to life at almost any age. A key element in this balance is faith, which transcends the rational mind and draws upon the deep intuitive forces within to help one have strength for the present and hope for the future. In many areas of life we live by faith and to recognize this and to feed faith encourages imagination, and creativity, and enables us to take those risks that are necessary for good growth.

Positive attitudes about God provide perspectives for persons. Perspective, which is to see life through spectacles that have a wide vision and a long view, promotes patience and posits priorities and values which are important in child development.

Inspiration, a basic factor in genius, literally means to breathe in. The biblical understanding of inspiration is that of the Spirit breathing in life and creativity. It is the one who is awake and open to the Spirit who experiences inspiration that guides and goads genius to progress and perfection. It is this same inspiration that provides power to persist, strength to survive and courage to make commitments.

Purpose and meaning in life are important for bringing genius to fruition. Faith in God always involves purpose and meaning, no matter what one's religion is. In every religion the believer strives to understand and appropriate God's will for himself. It is God's will that provides the basis for our own will, our own choices, and thereby establishes purpose and meaning for our lives. "Commit your labors to the Lord and your plans will be established," says the writer of the Old Testament book of Proverbs. (16:3)

Positive attitudes about God thus provide a relationship with an ultimate source and force that helps us establish and clarify goals, set priorities and receive direction for holistic living. Integration of selfhood is facilitated and intentional living is fostered. Although children may not recognize these dynamics, it is important for parents to see these values of faith in God.

God is Spirit and to recognize and root our lives in Spirit is to be open to the operation and influence of spiritual forces. Those non-rational and non-physical phenomena that frequently occur in

childhood and which open windows to other realities and to exciting, expansive living, are fostered by faith in God. These phenomena include clairvoyance, clairaudience, clairsentience, telepathy, communication with the spirit world and elementals, precognition, out-of-body travel and other extra-sensory activity.
Values, morals, and ethics are largely derived from spiritual and religious systems and beliefs. To recognize a Supreme Law-giver can be the beginning of respect for others and reverence for life at all levels. When God is a recognized and experienced reality in human lives, families, communities, societies and civilizations are more likely to survive and flourish.
Positive attitudes about God nurture love. It is God's love, expressed by all religions, that enables us to love others and ourselves. Love is essential for wholeness. Love brings faith and sustains genius; enriches, ennobles, and enables life at all levels. The quality and expression of love in our lives is primarily, though not always recognized or admitted, the result of our giving and receiving love from God, who is the Source of all love.

Some specific exercises for developing positive attitudes about God

The possibilities for conceiving and experiencing God are endless. Generally, we conceive and experience God through personal awareness of the divine presence consciously interpreted as such. This often happens in corporate worship, private devotions, prayer, meditation, through the sacraments or in mystical moments. Or we may conceive and experience God through the whole range of human activities — physical, mental, emotional, aesthetic, social, economic, political, etc. — where these are seen in some way as manifestations of God's involvement in human history. A third possibility is conceiving and experiencing God's presence and power in a wide variety of intimations of transcendence, e.g., in nature, in which there is a feeling, a sensing of the divine, but no clear revelation.

The following thoughts and exercises represent some possibilities or models that can be helpful for children and adults in conceiving and experiencing God in any of the above three ways.

1. God sometimes becomes more real to us as we use familiar metaphors and then relate these to our thoughts and feelings about God. For example, consider the questions: How do you think of God — as a raging storm or a quiet lake? As a gentle companion or a powerful ruler? As a consuming fire or a bubbling stream? In this exercise, best done in a group, after the choices are made, you can discuss why you made a certain choice. Such discussions can bring interesting insights about the dynamics of God in the universe and in your own life.
2. Children ask about the nature and function of God. You can answer sometimes through images such as a fish swimming in the sea. We are the fish, God is the sea — powerful, majestic, dynamic, unfathomable — which furnishes food, provides the medium in which we function and moves in and through us providing the breath of life.
3. Statements such as those below, in which you answer yes or no, provide a stimulus for discussions about God. For young children, sim-

pler statements or ones more relevant to their experiences can be used.
— God is very real to me in my daily living.
— Prayer is a great help to me and keeps my faith alive.
— I trust God with my innermost feelings and thoughts.
— My active participation in the church is important to God.
— God speaks to me most clearly in Sunday worship and Church School.
— God is far removed from this evil world.
— God speaks to me significantly through the Bible.
— God has a specific plan for my life.
— God helps me in my suffering.

4. Nature provides an excellent medium for a child's introduction to God. With a little imagination, the possibilities are copious. Sunsets, snowflakes, baby animals, insects, flowers, water and so many other natural phenomena offer examples anytime during the year. Even complex church doctrines can sometimes be clarified through examples from nature. Thus the Christian doctrine of the Trinity (Father, Son and Holy Spirit) can be discussed in terms of three forms of water — solid, liquid, gas — where the substance is the same but the forms differ.

5. Art and music also can be used in numerous ways to help one get in touch with ideas and feelings about the divine. Having children draw or paint pictures about God or creating songs about God, and then discussing their creations,

ATTITUDES ABOUT GOD

often brings forth some surprising and unique revelations about God and the child.
6. Considering statements about death and life after death can bring insights about God. In having children answer yes or no to the following, and then talking about their thoughts and feelings in their answers, you can clarify ideas about God and allay doubts or fears that often accompany consideration of death.
   — My life continues forever after death.
   — I fear death.
   — God utterly destroys the wicked after death.
   — Prayers for the departed ones are important.
   — I believe there is development and progress after death.
   — My relationship to God now is important for life after death.
   — I want to survive after death.
7. The subject of birth and babies always fascinates children. As you answer their questions about the process of life in the womb, birth and infancy, try to relate your comments to God's creative processes, his love and care and the precious and sacred nature of life.
8. For the Christian, the life and teachings of Jesus provide one of the best approaches to attitudes about God. All persons can identify with a human being. To transfer the qualities of the life of Jesus to God is a good way to help children obtain understanding of and appreciation for God. This approach necessitates some sound knowledge of the Bible, which is certainly a major source for conceiving and experiencing God. In fact, this is what the Bible is all about — the record of the mighty acts of God in human history and how persons have con-

ceived of and experienced God in their personal and corporate lives. This also is true for the Scriptures of other religions. No adequate understanding or appreciation of God can be taught or caught without some serious study of the scriptures of religions. Daily memory verses from scripture about God provide powerful energies and good guidance for wholesome living.

9. Finally, you can reflect on more profound thoughts about the mystery and love of God and about service to the Lord. The following is an example which contains a number of thoughts that can be separated out and used as meditation material.

The mystery of God is one of the clearest of His revelations. In His veiledness God unveils Himself. This unveiling through mystery has important implications for our knowing God. It means that we cannot be searching for God with preconceived ideas of who God is. To do this is to "staticize" our experience of His ever-newness to us. To live in the mystery of God is to know that the ages of sages are simply stages in the parting of the veil. Thus, we live according to highest probabilities rather than in the frustrating fragilities of the absolute certainty of knowing it all. God's mystery says that in history there will never be the demise of surprise for the cosmic kaleidoscope constantly turns and makes mosaics of meaning within the mystery. To live in the mystery of God creates that humility which brings tranquility to mind and spirit. To so live also brings responsibility and makes conscious our conscience. The mystery of God makes clear to us that we do not comprehend Him but that He apprehends and loves us forever.

The love of God is the source and goal of our being. To receive Divine Love is to be extinguished; to reflect Divine Love is to give eternal light. To receive God's love is to pass away; to share God's love is to endure forever. God's love is the genesis of all growth and change for His love ever calls us to leave the lesser for the greater to go on and on in perpetual discovery of His grandeur, glory and grace. To totally love God is to perform every act as a sacrament, with no concern for or expectation of results. To experience God's love is to experience the love for ourselves, for it is God's love for us that is the reason for us to love ourselves. We love ourselves only for God and we love each other for the same reason. Perfect love is God in the depths of our being, meeting God who comes to us. In this perfect love, this perfect communion, we know that all creation is nothing other than love.

To love God is to serve Him — serve Him with no expectation of wages, to serve Him not for fear of hell nor desire of heaven, but to serve Him for Himself alone. To serve God is to self-divest so that He may Self-invest. It is to one-point our lives so that our creed and deed agree with the seed of God within us. To rightly serve God is not just to act from facile fact but to trust in the "must" of His will and word; it is to rejoice in the choice He continually places before our faces and to gratefully expand and extend the whole of our being so that there can be the freeing of those found bound. To serve God is to move from tedium to *Te Deum*.

To be perfectly centered in God is not odd nor oblivion. For it is only when we are in the center of God's eye that we can be and say "I." It is then that the whole creation joins in the elation and celebration of our elevation to the Father's throne.

The Source of energy

Without sunlight, plants could not grow. Photosynthesis is the process by which plants create (synthesize) carbohydrates from water and carbon dioxide by the action of sunlight (photo) on the chlorophyll. Consequently, sunlight is the source of energy from which all living beings derive food for their bodies – plants creating carbohydrates from which both plants and animals (and man) derive their proteins and fats.

The human soul likewise requires nurturing from its source – God. As the sun feeds the earth, so does the Eternal Spirit feed the Soul with love and wisdom. As the flower turns to the sun to receive light for growth, so the Soul that turns to God receives light and love for its growth. Persistent positive attitudes and activities that center around God bring forth good fruits of the spirit that do not perish.

CHAPTER 4

MENTAL TRAINING: THE KEY TO PAT

General Aspects

Our brain functions as a highly sophisticated biocomputer. Whatever information we take in from our physical senses (sight, hearing, smell, taste, and touch) is indelibly imprinted in our memory bank. We are mainly visual animals: we believe more what we see than what we experience through any of the other senses. This is why our internal imagery is so important in establishing our belief, and hence our reality. The purpose of this chapter is to describe how the mind functions and to suggest mental exercises which are the keys to PAT.

The brain and the mind: are they the same?

Many people regard the mind and the brain as one and the same thing. Although they are dependent upon each other they are totally different.

The **brain** is an organ within our cranial vault. It is a physical entity having size, shape, mass and color. The brain emits frequencies which reflect the electrochemical activity going on within it. These brain wave frequencies are recordable on an electroencephalograph (EEG) machine. Everyone has four basic areas of these brain wave frequencies as shown in Figure 4-1. The four basic areas are: BETA, recordable from 14 to 32 cycles per second (cps); ALPHA, 8-13 cps; THETA, 4-7 cps; and DELTA, 0.3-3 cps. These will be discussed later.

The mind, on the other hand, is an abstract entity which reflects through the physical brain. The mind cannot be truly measured any more than electricity can be measured. However, we know it exists. Electrical power cannot be contained but, with certain rules in operation, it can be controlled. The power of the mind operates similarly.

One aspect of the mind is reflected and measurable on an I.Q. (intelligence quotient) test. Some would argue that measurement of the I.Q. is limiting and what we should be considering is P.Q. (i.e., potential quotient). The truth is now emerging that the mind has almost infinite capabilities.

We need to appreciate the fact that we do have a mind existing within this body-mind-spirit unit and that our mind is most powerful. Because of the power it has, we should be aware of what is contained within it and what we are continuously putting in it as thought forms.

How the mind functions

As noted, our brain (and mind) functions as a highly sophisticated biocomputer. With man-made computers it is well known that what comes out reflects what goes in. Logic in, logic out. Garbage in, garbage out. The same is true for our minds.

What enters our minds as children will be reflected throughout our lives as adults.

It **is** possible to change deeply-ingrained concepts and habits, but considerable energy and effort is required to do so. We acknowledge this energy when we refer to individuals as having **will power** to change a particular pattern about themselves.

It would be ideal, of course, to have learned good habits in the first place. This is what PAT is all about. The process involves using the conscious mind to train the subconscious mind to be our trusted servant.

The conscious and subconscious minds

We have two minds — conscious and subconscious. The conscious mind works only during the times when we are awake and consciously aware. The brain is emitting predominately BETA wave frequencies. The conscious mind can, with great effort, override some subconscious events, such as habit control, but under ordinary circumstances it cannot influence others, such as heart rate, blood pressure, digestion, etc. The conscious mind can be trained to do more than it does. However, rather than letting it take on every little chore, it would be far better and more energy conserving to have the conscious mind train the subconscious mind.

The subconscious mind, on the other hand, works all the time, 24 hours a day. This part of the mind controls our breathing. It regulates our heart rate and blood pressure. It keeps our intestinal tract working to digest and assimilate food. It does these things without conscious thought. This is good.

If we were to use our conscious mind to keep our heart beating, what would happen if we remembered to take a breath? Our heart would stop! What would happen if we were to eat lunch and we had to use our conscious mind to control the digestive and assimilative processes? Our heart and breathing would stop! This may sound facetious, but it probably would be true. Whereas the conscious mind can usually direct only one operation at a time, the subconscious can perform many.

In addition, the subconscious mind is constantly working with information stored within the deeper recesses of our brain. From this complex interweaving of previously-stored thought forms, past experiences, and relationships, the mind creates our personality — a personality unique to each one of us.

When suddenly we are confronted with a new event, we respond automatically and very naturally in a way determined by our subconscious mind. It, therefore, becomes important what thought forms we put into our mind, because the subconscious part of the mind is going to draw from these stored thought forms to develop our own unique way of acting or reacting.

Some individuals are careful to create positive pictures and thoughts of love, understanding, tolerance, harmony, success, prosperity, a healthy self-image, etc., so that the subconscious mind has good wholesome ingredients with which to mold their personalities.

Others are not so careful. They create negative pictures and thoughts of anger, hatred, fear, jealousy, sorrow, anxiety, envy, intolerance, disharmony, failure, a poor self-image, etc. These individuals wonder why their mental strength is dissipated, why they experience tension and fatigue, why they develop destructive emotions, and even why they ultimately develop physical dis-ease. We must be aware of how powerful our minds really are. We must be aware of what we are putting into our minds for we really *reap what we sow,* that is, garbage in, garbage out. Let us teach our children through PAT to sow constructively so that they may reap constructively.

To return to a point made earlier about using the conscious mind to train the subconscious, it would be impractical to use the conscious mind to perform every little function. The conscious mind uses much energy, for it directs the whole body and the conscious mental energy to perform a particular event. The conscious mind functions at an energy state lower than the subconscious mind (Figure 4-1). Since using the subconscious mind conserves energy, why not train this automatic part of the mind to function the way we want it to?

Rather than teaching children to actively suppress what might be an automatic angry response of the subconscious, why not teach them to train their subconscious to automatically respond with tolerance? Instead of trying to actively suppress a fear, teach children to train their subconscious mind to develop confidence in their ability to overcome challenges. The subconscious mind can be a great asset if used correctly. It's like having a great army of minds to rally to our needs. However, it must be developed and trained. PAT is designed to employ the conscious mind to train the subconscious to be positive, constructive and uplifting so that this behavior becomes habit and will predominate throughout life.

Exciting information from mind/brain research: right vs. left brain

The brain is a most interesting organ. The abstract entity we call the mind is even more fascinating. Researchers are now discovering that both sides of our brain do not function in the same way. We apparently have a right brain and a left brain, a right mind and a left mind!

Most of us know that one side of the brain controls the muscles on the opposite side of the body: the right side of the brain (RB) controls the left side of the body, the left side of the brain (LB) controls the right side. The anatomical reason is that at the base of the brain the nerve fiber tracts cross over. Usually, one side of the brain is dominant in these matters: most individuals are right-handed indicating LB dominance; few people are left-handed indicating RB dominance. Usually one can observe a subtle enlargement of the muscles on the dominant side, probably because they are used more. Although there are a few individuals who appear to be ambidextrous (they use either hand equally well), you can detect a slight difference indicating their preference to use one hand.

In an individual who is right-sided and whose LB is dominant, the LB is associated with logical thinking, deductive reasoning, mathematics, information derived from the physical sense, etc. The RB of these individuals is associated with non-spatial events, psychic talents (e.g., ESP, precognition, psychokinesis, telepathy, probably healing), creative dreaming, inventing, poetry writing, art, etc. With the lefthanded individuals these conditions may be reversed: the RB concerned with logical thinking; the LB with psychic non-spatial talents.

Our society and educational system concentrates on developing the LB of an individual, slowly but surely making the RB more inactive from disuse. Children who are talented in the arts are compelled to excel in mathematics. Little is done to teach them to develop their creative RB talents. Later in life, when they are searching for the true meaning of life, they are unable to use that part of their mind which is concerned with these thoughts and with creative thinking. They have suppressed RB activity so much that it becomes a real chore to recover from the years of stagnation.

The brain and mind function as any other organ and talent we may have. The more we use the faculty of memory, the better we are able to memorize. When I was taking second-year college English, my professor made us memorize poetry all year long. We started with 10- to 15-line poems, and the last poem we had to memorize was Francis Thompson's *The Hound of Heaven,* all 183 lines of it! Believe it or not, it was easier to memorize the 183 lines of this poem than it was 20 lines of a poem given us in the beginning of the year. Our professor admitted at the end of the course that the poems he gave us to memorize were not all that important. What he wanted us to do was develop our faculty of memory. He believed that the more we use such a faculty, the better it would function. He was correct.

The more we use and develop our psychic talents, the better we are able to use these aspects of our mind for self-analysis, self-development, and any degree of self-help, including self-health. This is essentially what this book is about: teaching children and young adults through PAT to develop their inner self for growth, development and creative living. I believe these are RB functions and children can be taught to further develop these talents of the RB and mind by using PAT techniques of affirmation, meditation, and positive mental imagery.

Mental activities related to brain waves and states of consciousness

The mind is a source of energy and it is this MIND POWER which we can use to control all aspects of not only our physical bodies but also our mental and emotional responses.

The brain emits frequencies which reflect the electrochemical activity going on within it. Scientists have been able to detect four basic areas of brain wave frequencies as determined by EEG recordings (Figure 4-1).

One area is called BETA. This is a fast frequency range with low energy potential recordable from 14-32 cps. This is the brain wave frequency we use to see, hear, smell, taste, and touch. Essentially, when the normal individual is awake and functioning at the outer **conscious** level, BETA wave frequencies are emitted.

The second area, termed ALPHA and recordable from 8-13 cps, is one of the three frequency ranges emitted during sleep and while dreaming. This level is also called REM sleep because while dreaming we have rapid eye movement. ALPHA range frequencies, which are slower and more energetic than BETA, are also emitted during meditation and self-hypnosis.

The third area, called THETA and recordable from 4-7 cps, is even slower and more energetic than BETA and ALPHA. THETA brain wave frequencies are detected during sleep and also during deeper states of meditation and self-hypnosis.

The fourth area, DELTA, recordable from 0.3-3 cps, is the state an individual is in while in deepest sleep, coma, and deep anesthesia. It is possible to reach DELTA during hypnosis but not very likely through self-hypnosis. Some believe that it may be possible to reach DELTA by meditation, but this requires considerable practice and extraordinary discipline. An important feature about the DELTA state is that while individuals may appear to be unconscious, in deepest sleep, coma, or deep anesthesia, they may be able to hear and record onto their brain cells what they heard while in this state. Although they will not have any **awareness** of what they heard, it still is recorded and will influence their subconscious thinking afterwards.

Schematically in Figure 4-1, I assigned the so-called **unconscious** state to DELTA. Even though I have done this, I am not convinced that there is any such state as the unconscious! I believe that man is involved with three states or levels of consciousness, namely the conscious, subconscious and superconscious. Under ordinary circumstances the BETA brain wave reflects the conscious state and the ALPHA, THETA, and DELTA brain waves reflect gradations of the subconscious state. Because these latter three brain-wave areas represent high-level energy states, they are probably employed to link man with the **superconscious** realm. More details about this await a future volume.

Let us consider the relationship between the states of consciousness and mental energy. The conscious mind functions at the lowest level of mental energy. This is understandable. It takes energy to run the machine: to move muscles and to employ the physical senses. It is reasonable to assume that during these times of high physical energy utilization, the residual pure mental energy or Mind Power would be low, as it appears to be.

During sleep our brain waves fluctuate from 13 all the way down to 0.3 cps. In fact, every 90 minutes of sleep our brain waves fluctuate from DELTA through THETA to ALPHA as depicted in Table 4-1. REM sleep is the most energetic form of sleep and man spends more time in REM sleep each night than in any of the other sleep states. Even though we are not conscious during sleep, our mental energy is high. This may be one reason why we are able to dream during this state.

In my opinion, the THETA area reflects the **subconscious** state at a level where habits are programmed. It is significant to note that habits are deep-seated programs existing at a level of mental activity considerably higher than our conscious mind. The reason that most individuals make New Year's resolutions which are doomed to failure (usually by January 2nd) is that they are trying to change a high-energy program by using their lowest energy mental state. It would be like trying to move a boxcar using your little finger. Failure makes sense when we consider the energy involved.

It would be more reasonable to attempt to employ THETA energy to change habits, to use locomotive energy to move the boxcar. Then we would have a greater chance of success.

But, of what use is this stronger ALPHA and THETA energy if we are ordinarily sleeping while

BRAINWAVE FREQUENCIES

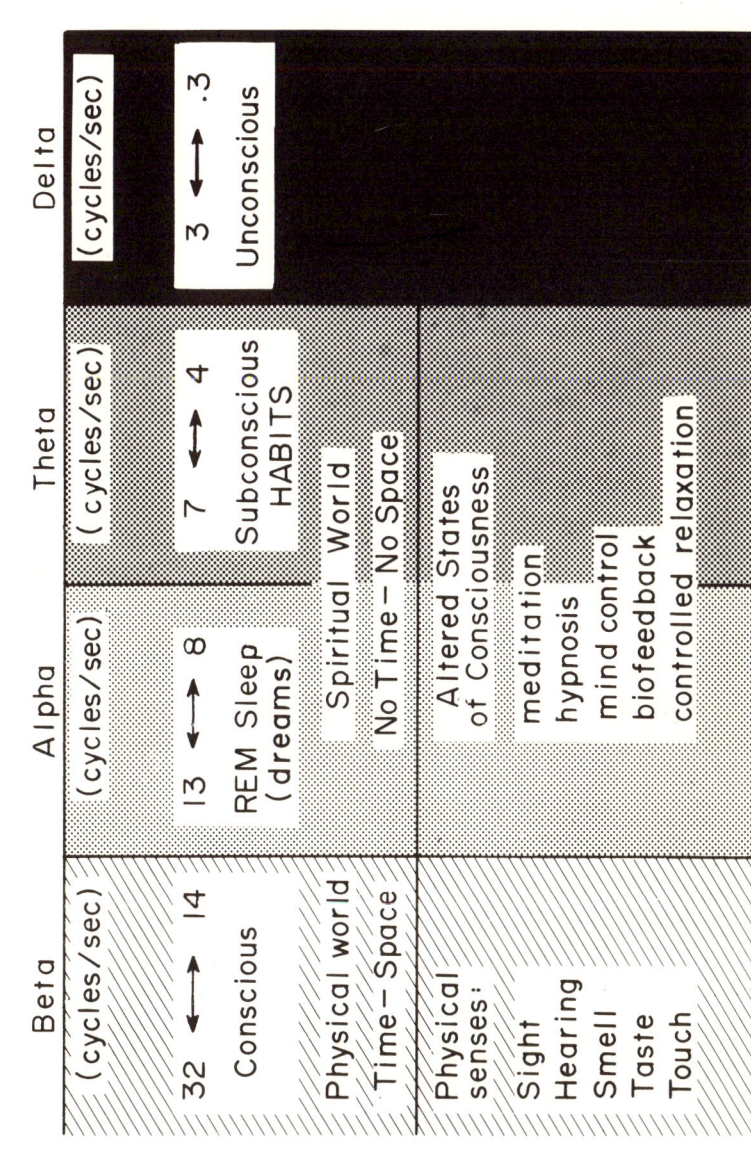

Beta	Alpha	Theta	Delta
(cycles/sec)	(cycles/sec)	(cycles/sec)	(cycles/sec)
32 ↔ 14	13 ↔ 8	7 ↔ 4	3 ↔ .3
Conscious	REM Sleep (dreams)	Subconscious HABITS	Unconscious
Physical world Time – Space	Spiritual World No Time – No Space		
Physical senses: Sight Hearing Smell Taste Touch	Altered States of Consciousness meditation hypnosis mind control biofeedback controlled relaxation		

Figure 4-1

these energy states exist? Because we are not conscious during sleep we are unable to direct this energy to achieve our goal.

However, the Creator has provided ways of achieving these high-energy mental states with conscious awareness. An individual is in an Altered State of Consciousness when he has achieved the state of ALPHA, THETA, or DELTA with conscious awareness. Techniques employed to reach these altered states include meditation, hypnosis, mind control, biofeedback, and controlled, progressive relaxation, to name a few. These techniques are **all** the same; they all achieve the same results. The differences exist only in the minds of those teaching the particular exercise.

During meditation and self-hypnosis the brain emits ALPHA or THETA brain wave frequencies, depending upon how deep the individual is within these states. The ALPHA and THETA brain wave frequencies are slower, more stable, and more energetic than the BETA level frequencies. We now know that we can reach the ALPHA and THETA levels while being consciously aware and that we can employ these stronger, more energetic brain wave frequencies with **conscious awareness** to control bodily functions and to change habits. Equally exciting is the realization that we can at will experience the ALPHA level to achieve inner peace of mind and tranquility. Conscious mind power can involve an unlimiting process.

Increasing mental strength lies in our ability to enter the altered states of consciousness with conscious awareness. These states exist within a rather narrow range of brain wave frequencies, and discipline is required not only to reach these areas but also to maintain awareness while there.

MENTAL TRAINING THE KEY TO PAT

Useful reference points to appreciate the normal range of brain wave frequencies would be to realize that zero represents a dead brain and at 60 cps an individual is having a convulsion. There are two situations we encounter almost daily which keep us focused towards the 60-cps end — the opposite direction we need to go to relax and achieve increased mental strength.

Fluorescent lights flicker at 60 cps in tune with the 60 cps vibration of alternating current. We have known the deleterious effect fluorescent lighting has upon individuals who spend considerable time exposed to this type of lighting and deprived of natural sunlight. This is especially noticeable in the winter months when individuals leave their homes early in the morning before the sun rises and return home late, after the sun has gone down. Tension and stress increase considerably during mid-and late-winter and begin to subside as the days get longer in the spring.

Another device which flickers at 60 cps is TV and for the same reason. In fact, watching TV has triggered convulsions in epileptic-prone individuals. Not only are the average TV programs negative, but the 60 cps flicker keeps individuals focused in the direction opposite to that where inner mental strength exists. As mentioned earlier, we are mainly visual animals and we very easily tune into light vibrations. These facts need to be considered as we evaluate a total program of PAT for children.

Encephalographers (individuals who interpret EEGs) generally agree that EEG machines detect brain waves coming from the outer *cortex*, the so-called *grey matter* of the brain and the seat of our conscious mental functions.

The subconscious mind is centered in deeper levels, probably the so-called *limbic* and *reticular* areas, supposedly beyond the reach of these instruments. Although there appears to be a correlation between what goes on in the outer *cortex* and the *limbic* and *reticular* areas, it is not total. This is the reason why the hypnotic state cannot be defined by EEG readings.

It is unreasonable to assume that all brain waves detected by the EEG machine come from the *cortex* of the brain. There is considerable electrical activity going on at deeper levels and it probably picks them up. How to separate those waves coming from deeper levels from those arising from the more superficial areas and determining their significance is far beyond the scope of this book. It is conceivable that only BETA waves emanate from the *cortex* and ALPHA, THETA, and DELTA waves come from deeper levels.

The three keys to mind power

Mind power is effective when three criteria are fulfilled: the proper and constructive use of our imagination, the development and use of our powers of visualization, and the degree to which we believe it, i.e., our belief factor.

Our imaginations create the thoughts which are processed through our biocomputer. These mental images not only influence our everyday behavior, but also become integral parts of us. Since we become what we imagine ourselves to be, it becomes important for us to be creative and positive in our imagination. A positive creative imagery will cause us to be positive, creative and more constructive. Conversely, a negative imagery will result in our being negative and destructive.

Since our mind believes most what it sees, our ability to visualize mentally further reinforces what is being channeled. It is reasonable to conclude that developing our power of visualization adds impetus to our (positive or negative) creative imaginings.

Furthermore, believing in what we create and visualize convinces the mind. Our subconscious inner belief system (i.e., our belief factor) is the important one, and this may be different from what we think we believe consciously. As mentioned earlier, **belief creates reality.** Through meditation we can be taught to know our inner beliefs, and, therefore, we will begin to know ourselves.

PAT consists of teaching children and young adults to develop positive creative imageries, to learn internal mental imagery, and to create a positive constructive and uplifting inner subconscious belief in themselves. All this is achievable and, from experience, a worthwhile effort.

Obstacles to growth

There are basically two obstacles to growth, namely, ignorance and resistance to change.

In my experience teaching our Center's T-H-E-M-E Mental Training Seminar for adults, I have been fortunate to have observed many individuals solve the particular challenges which attracted them to the seminars in the first place. In all cases those who succeed enter the program with an **open** mind and a sincere commitment to their goal. As they enter with the desire to be enlightened, they become enlightened. Even though some may fear change initially, this fear is replaced with strength as they progress along in the training.

I also have made it a point to observe the failures and thus far most of those who fail do so because they cannot get beyond their *ignorance* and *resistance to change.*

It is through ignorance that individuals often fail to realize that God has made **all** things possible for those who believe in Him and in themselves. We must believe that God has given us everything we need to create our own reality. Anything short of that would be an admission that God shortchanged us. The Universe is infinite and the bounty equally plentiful. We must overcome ignorance, sit at the banquet table, and believe that the meal is served.

Resistance to change is the other great obstacle preventing individuals from achieving success. Observing individuals who desire to, but do not, succeed reveals that generally the resistance to change is stronger than the willingness to make a change. We are a society which values stability and security, two nails in the coffin of life. Everything in the Universe is in constant change: the galaxies, solar systems, planets, minerals, plant and animal life. Even atoms making up what would appear to be the most inert matter are teeming with electron and atomic energy. Energy itself by definition is constantly moving. When we seek stability, we are going counter to all of the forces of nature. Individuals who resist change are dead spirits waiting to be buried.

When we learn as children to accept that all expressions of God are dynamic and that human expression and life itself depends upon change as a vital essence, we do not fear change. In fact, we learn to welcome it.

PAT helps children learn to welcome knowledge and to become aware of and avoid ignorance. In addition, they learn to accept change as a vital expression of everything which exists in the world. With this realization they will gradually overcome the fear of change.

The four keys of self-development and self-realization

Every organ within the body functions according to the laws governing it. Medical science has accumulated considerable knowledge about the anatomy, physiology, and biochemistry of the heart, lungs, stomach, intestines, kidneys, etc. Considerable is known about the anatomy and biochemistry of the brain. Obtaining concrete data on how thought forms and ideas originate, get stored in memory, and are retrieved when needed has been more difficult to obtain.

Much of what we know represents theories and hypotheses which appear to work when put into practice. The important thing is that, if it works, why not use it to expand knowledge.

The mind functions like no other entity within the body. Maybe it is because it is one of the two abstract entities within us. (The other is spirit-life itself and medical science knows even less about that!) We have already discussed the three keys to mind power, but these do not explain how to use the mind for self-development and self-realization. I believe that four keys are operative here.

Self-responsibility. The situation that puts the subconscious on the alert that we mean business is the firm commitment that we will assume self-responsibility for all of our actions toward a particular goal, that is, all 100 percent. Once we think we have done this, the tricky subconscious begins to test us. We might even hear it asking: are you sure you didn't mean 95 percent, or perhaps 90 percent, or maybe 50 percent? Unless it is 100 percent, changing a habit of behavior may still be difficult.

A gentleman who once completed one of our T-H-E-M-E Training Seminars told me that it wasn't until he made a total 100 percent commitment to what he wanted to believe that the welcomed changes began to occur. In other words, it wasn't until he transposed what he wanted to believe to what he truly believed, not until it became a subconscious inner belief, that the positive belief began to create the positive reality.

How many individuals tell themselves they are going to start dieting on Monday but never do? (I always facetiously quip that they never tell their subconscious which Monday!) The subconscious part of us is a willing servant and acts according to the direction it receives, whether clear or vague. If we are phony, our subconscious knows us for what we are. If we are sincerely determined, it knows that also.

Actions do speak louder than words. When actions team with thoughts and words, the subconscious is impressed in triplicate and begins to demonstrate the order placed. It is action that crystallizes thought into reality. When we say that we are going to do something, let us take the first step and do it. Indicate to our subconscious that we are ready and that **it** better be ready or else!

Using positive affirmation is one way of reinforcing a commitment to the subconscious self. By using meditation one can tap the inner Mind Power and talk with the Subconscious (in THETA) on an equal footing.

Self-awareness. By developing an increasing awareness about ourselves we gradually heighten our level of consciousness to the point at which we know more of **who** we are, **where** we came from, **why** we do the things we do, and **where** we are going. This quest for self-awareness continues as long as there is life within the body. Some believe that the soul continues this quest long after physical life, as we know it, ceases.

By using meditation (in ALPHA), we can communicate with that part of us which represents our highest ideals. We can communicate with God through prayer (a form of meditation) to guide us toward an increasing realization of who we are and what is really important. As our awareness increases, we will begin to know why we smoke, why we overeat, why we are tense and fearful, etc. More importantly, we are ready to develop the next key.

Self-control is the key with which we carefully monitor the what, where, when and how of our life. We sit as master at the controls of our mental central communications center. When we decide that now is the time to execute a desired action, we can eventually press the button and *presto* it is done!

We can be in control of our emotions by carefully balancing the polarity of any emotion. We can then effect positive uplifting results accordingly.

One way to start gaining self-control is through the use of affirmations at any level of consciousness. When using the meditative process, we can see ourselves before a console containing knobs and dials for the various physical, mental and spiritual aspects of our being that we wish to direct, and then see ourselves orchestrating the symphony of choice.

Self-discipline. The key to developing control over our subconscious is discipline. We boost our chances immensely in attaining the changes we want. Without it our inner mind will not take us seriously.

We have encountered numerous individuals who have desired to change habits of behavior, ostensibly assuming total responsibility, and seemingly increasing the areas of awareness and control, but changes apparently do not occur. In other words, their subconscious is deaf to their desires. Employing techniques to develop self-discipline results in achieving their goals.

There is no better way to perk up the ears of the subconscious than by discipline.

Self-discipline is the key to controlling not only your physical senses but also your whole life. Self-discipline usually requires training the body. You do not have to abuse or torture yourself, although these extremes have worked with some individuals throughout history. We do not recommend it. Self-mutilation is not and should not be one of our aims. Self-discipline is rather the state you are in when your body, mind, and spirit are finely tuned to each other, with the mind and spirit in control. When you have achieved this state, you experience joy and happiness.

Have you ever watched a spoiled child or an untrained animal? It is possible they have a lot in common! The spoiled child is never satisfied. The more you give him, the more he wants. He is always manipulating others to get his way, and, when he does, he is still unhappy. He is usually grumpy all the time. An untrained animal is much the same way — never relaxed, uptight, constantly seeking attention, etc.

Well-trained animals are usually happy ones. Watch as they perform with their heads held high, proud of themselves, and if they could smile you would be able to see that too. Well-disciplined children are also happy. They are proud of themselves and derive a great deal of satisfaction from their accomplishments.

Learning self-discipline may be different for adults and children. Adults could benefit from fasting, praying, and denial of something they physically and psychologically enjoy.

Young children can learn the benefits of self-discipline by observing the example of their parents and by using affirmations. Older children can learn to employ prayer and denial. Young adults may voluntarily add fasting to the list of useful techniques.

Superlearning

Important to the process of *awakening the genius* is the concept of **superlearning.** In the mid-1960s a group of Bulgarian scientists under the inspiration and direction of Dr. Georgi Lozanov investigated a rather unique learning system whereby individuals could be taught to learn and remember vast quantities of information quickly, effectively and effortlessly. Although these studies were initiated at the Institute of Suggestology in Sophia, Bulgaria, they are being continued, and expanded and refined elsewhere.

Mind scientists throughout the world now realize that we are presently functioning at a very low level of our mental capacities, that we are beginning to discover the virtually limitless capacities of the mind, that by conscious command we are able to evolve cerebral centers which will permit us to use powers we are now not even capable of imagining, and that the brain has an almost infinite creative capacity.

Dr. Lozanov is convinced from his research that we already have super-memory. The problem is that we do not easily recall what we store away. If we were able to present information to our mental biocomputer under ideal circumstances, the brain would absorb vast quantities of knowledge and information, and we would be able to retrieve more of this information when we so desire. Studies reveal that by employing super-memory techniques an average individual is able to learn 1,000 new vocabulary words of a foreign language in eight hours of such training. And, this can be accomplished rather effortlessly. This fact alone, if applied, could revolutionize the educational field.

Lozanov believes that *relaxation* and *suggestion* are the bases of super-memory. He calls his learning system *suggestopedia,* which is a branch of the much larger discipline of *suggestology.* Important to superlearning are a number of things, such as rhythm, breathing, music, and meditative (relaxation) states.

Suggestology essentially is *active* meditation, a state of relaxation wherein the individual actively forms mental pictures of the events he or she desires to compute or experience: it could be words or a lesson to be memorized; or correcting an ill-health situation, such as hypertension, ulcers, or pain; or altering a behavior condition such as hyperactivity, nervous tension, or uncontrolled anger emotions; or correcting learning disabilities such as poor concentration and attentiveness, or dyslexia; or it could be attempting to achieve a goal in life. *Active* meditation or *suggestology* attempts to coordinate left-brain and right-brain activities with body functions in a way to make individuals more capable of achieving whatever they are trying to do.

In addition to employing these techniques to improve and heal dis-ease conditions and to enhance factual learning, suggestology appears to open up the intuitive, creative, and extrasensory abilities of individuals.

Ostrander and co-authors in their book on *Super-Learning* (Delacorte Press/Confucian Press, New York, 1979) describe these new stress-free, fast-learning methods which can be used to develop super-memory and improve business and sports performance. Parents and teachers interested in learning more are advised to read this very important and provocative book.

If superlearning techniques can help individuals improve memory and physical performance, then, with slight modification, these same techniques could be used to improve children's attitudes about themselves. We employ superlearning techniques to teach children not only to improve their learning, but also, and probably more importantly, to help them develop positive attitudes and improve their self-images. As part of our T-H-E-M-E Positive Attitude Training Camps, children are taught in class using rhythm, music, and relaxation. They listen to positive affirmations until these become a part of their thinking. Once they view themselves at the subconscious level as succeeding, they are ready to act accordingly. They are given special cassette tapes which they (and their parents) can use at home for reinforcement. Once children improve their self-esteem and self-image, they are happy. This is reflected in their improved learning and performance.

Although the I.Q. of an individual is thought to be a fixed statement of one's intelligence, the P.Q.

seems almost limitless. It is to this description of a child's potential that *Awaken the Genius* is directed.

Summary

Mental training is the key to PAT. The brain functions as a highly sophisticated biocomputer. The mind which runs our whole existence is an abstract entity functioning through the physical brain. The quality of the thoughts and ideas coming out of our mind and brain is directly related to the quality of the thought forms created and stored, especially during our early developing years as infants and children. Initially, thoughts are created by the conscious part of the mind, and then stored in the biocomputer memory bank. Later much of what is created and executed becomes a product of our automatic subconscious mind. Since the subconscious mind functions from a very high state of mental energy (as compared to the conscious which functions from the lowest), it becomes prudent to retrain the subconscious early to create positive attitude habits. Techniques of affirmation to create positive creative imaginings, of meditation to tap the high-energy mind power of the subconscious mind, and of positive mental imagery to impress what is desired deep into the inner subconscious belief system are a part of PAT, and when employed early in life, are more effective than when they are used later in life after the subconscious has already developed bad thought habits. The four keys of self-development and self-realization (i.e., self-responsibility, self-awareness, self-control, and self-discipline) are important elements in communicating desires to the subconscious and having them executed in the way we want them to be.

The garden architect

The most fruitful gardens are those that are conceived and planted with vision and order. Throwing out seeds haphazardly in the field yields a low-level harvest. A properly-conceived plan provides the conditions necessary for germination of the seed and growth and development of the plant, allowing for sufficient watering, sunlight and food. Orderly planting involves proper spacing so that each plant has enough room to have sufficient nutrients.

The key to developing positive attitudes and awakening the genius is proper mental training. Such training requires order, planning, and space for the flower and fruit of the germinal genius to unfold.

CHAPTER 5

POSITIVE ATTITUDE TRAINING (PAT) TECHNIQUES

Introduction

It is an acknowledged fact, that if you wish to develop your muscles, you must exercise them. The more you exercise them, the larger and stronger they become. On the other hand, if you do not use a muscle for any length of time, it atrophies, that is, it shrinks. Each individual muscle fiber gets smaller and weakens.

If you desire to become proficient at any particular sport (e.g., golf, tennis, baseball, etc.), the more you practice, the more proficient you become.

Functions of the brain and mind are no different. I already recounted the story of my college English professor who assigned us poetry to memorize during the year. He wanted us to develop our faculty of memory, and we did by memorizing poetry. He believed that the more an individual used such a mental faculty, the greater it would function. The results supported his belief.

The more we use and develop our psychic talents, the better we are able to use these aspects of our mind for self-analysis, self-development, and any degree of self-help, including self-health. This is essentially what PAT is designed to accomplish.

We **can** develop our minds to accomplish the goals listed in Chapter 1. But **how** can this be accomplished?

Through mental games. When introducing PAT techniques to children, we present them as games. Unlike adults, children are always receptive and willing to play games. Some adults, on the other hand, consider the games silly. This attitude seriously destroys their belief and interferes with learning. For this reason we believe that PAT is considerably more effective in children than in adults. Our experiences in our Center's T-H-E-M-E Positive Attitude Training Camps support this belief.

This chapter describes three of the most important techniques which can be employed for PAT in children and young adults. Obviously the use of these same procedures is beneficial to adults and is required if they wish to use them with their children. In fact after children undergo PAT in our camp setting, parents are instructed by the use of manuals and tapes how to reinforce the training at home. This chapter can only serve as a brief description of techniques which are described in more detail in another volume, *Manual of Positive Attitude Training (PAT) Techniques for Children and Young Adults,* by Nicola M. Tauraso, M.D., 1981, Hidden Valley Press, Frederick, Maryland.

Affirmation

Affirmation to develop positive belief factor. Affirmation is one of the key ways of changing estab-

POSITIVE ATTITUDE TRAINING (PAT) TECHNIQUES 67

lished belief patterns, of convincing your subconscious that you mean business, and of developing a positive *belief* factor. We have already mentioned that your *belief* factor is one of the three keys to mental power and success in accomplishing goals. We will now discuss the significance of *belief* in developing positive attitudes.

Just how important is *belief* and *faith* in the use of mind power? From my observations, I would conclude that without believing, the use of your imagination and power of visualization is almost useless! **It is *belief* which supplies the real power behind the workings of the subconscious. *Belief* creates reality.** We've seen this demonstrated over and over again in our T-H-E-M-E Training Seminars for adults and in our individual counselings. In fact, even a dull imagaination and a vague visualization effort can often be offset by a powerful *belief* system. Many individuals have accomplished great physical and mental feats by knowing the power of *belief* and faith.

If you do not believe in the images you create and visualize (i.e., your imagery), your mind will not be totally convinced. If this be the case, your mind power will be wasted and ineffective. Your subconscious *belief* system is the important one, and this may be different from what you think you believe consciously.

Researchers have shown that memory, concentration, success, creativity, leadership, other mental, and even physical conditions are not related to what an individual states is his *belief* about his particular mental or physical challenge, but rather are **directly** related to his ***inner belief*** about it. In most cases an individual's ***inner belief*** becomes increasingly hidden from him as he gets older, unless he actively cultivates increasing self-awareness. An individual's *inner belief* can be and has been brought to light through meditation and self-hypnosis.

As mentioned earlier, the inner subconscious is operating all the time, 24 hours a day. Your conscious mind works only during those times when you are consciously thinking about a particular event. Children and young adults can be taught to use their conscious minds to train their subconscious so that their inner subconscious will reflect what they consciously desire. Positive affirmations are designed to achieve this goal.

Belief Affirmations. Start by developing a series of **Belief Affirmations** that will establish for your children a way of living. You may modify the affirmations presented below. However, insure that they are stated in a positive manner.

1. I believe in the existence of God, a higher power, a force of love, that is eternal and puts meaning into our lives.
2. I believe that I have the mind-power to gain and maintain control over all of my life forces, both mind and body.
3. I believe that my own life force is an extension of the God force working within me and through me.
4. Since the God force is all-powerful, then the life force within me is all-powerful.
5. I believe that I can improve my life by improving my way of thinking.
6. I believe that I can acquire, experience, and maintain inner peace of mind.
7. I believe that life is worth living, that I am an instrument of the God force to do good.
8. I believe that love begins with me, that I can give love, accept love, and share love.

9. I believe that I can conquer any bad habit detrimental to my mental and physical health and I can develop and maintain good health habits.
10. I believe that the God power within me can make my life more successful, and ever better, better, and better.
11. I believe that I am master of my fate and that life is what I make it.

I would like to call your attention to Affirmations 1 to 4. Our subconscious mind is very logical. It is for this reason that we experience either success or limiting experiences, wellness or dis-ease, happiness or sadness, love or hate. Our minds and bodies will respond very logically to what exists as mental thought programs in our subconscious mind. It is what I call "mental cause and physical effect." Observe the progression of logic from "I believe in the existence of God..." to "I believe that I have the mind power..." to "I believe that my own life force is an extension of the God force..." to "Since the God force is all-powerful, then the life force within me is all-powerful." It would appear that one follows very naturally and logically from the preceeding affirmation. Our subconscious mind can and does accept this logic.

Use the affirmations daily with your children, twice daily if there is difficulty establishing a positive uplifting attitude. It is most important not to miss a day.

You will definitely begin to observe your children and yourself experiencing benefits from these affirmations. Many adult students remark that it appears simple. Yes, it is. However, it is not usually easy. These same students confirm that after having tried affirming they begin to see their life change for the better. Be aware that everyone is doing some form of affirming every day. The individual who says "I feel sick, I feel tired, my aching back, I can't think, I don't understand," etc., is affirming, but he is being negative about it. As authority figures, let us teach children and ourselves to **affirm only those things we wish to experience,** not the ones we don't.

Numerous individuals who have read our earlier book, *How to Benefit from Stress,* (by N. M. Tauraso and L. R. Batzler, 1979, Hidden Valley Press), in which some of these **Belief Affirmations** were first published, have written to say that they copied several affirmations, pasted them around the house (in the bedroom, bathroom, hallways, kitchen, refrigerator door, etc.), and would recite them every time they went by. Within days they found themselves transformed, running around the house full of energy when before they were tired and depressed. Isn't it amazing what the mind can do!

Plans for Living. The purpose of the **Plans for Living** statements is to teach children to establish important mini-goals in their lives. Take a few minutes each day and state these with your children as you do for the Belief Affirmations. I believe the **Plans for Living** are self-explanatory.

1. I have developed a zest for life.
2. I devote a portion of each day to improving my health.
3. I devote a portion of each day to improving my mind.
4. I engage in some form of moderate daily exercise.
5. I go to bed at a reasonable hour each night so that I always have adequate rest and sleep.
6. I observe common-sense rules about cleanli-

ness and wear clothes that enhance my outer appearance.
7. I take time each day for some form of recreation that relaxes me.
8. I devote a portion of each day to meditate upon the God force that works within me.
9. I remain young in mind and spirit.
10. I am positive and will associate and surround myself with positive uplifting people. Negative influences will not affect me.
11. I observe moderation in everything I do.
12. I practice controlled relaxation as a way of life.
13. I learn to grow wiser and more loving and compassionate toward fellow human beings.
14. I love life, I am glad to be alive, I have a will to live and I feel young.
15. Everyday in every way, I AM better, better, and better.
16. I am master of my fate and captain of my soul.

Affirmations for Developing Self-Responsibility

1. I am responsible for directing my whole life.
2. I am responsible for every aspect of my growth and development.
3. I am responsible for what I desire and for following through on my desires for improvement.
4. I am responsible for my habits, and I develop only good habits.
5. I am responsible for my thoughts and ideas.
6. I am responsible for what happens to me.
7. I am responsible for my own responsibility.
8. With God's help I am carrying out my responsibilities over myself.

Affirmations for Increasing Self-Awareness

1. My awareness over myself is getting greater and greater every day.
2. I know everything that happens to me.
3. I understand why things happen to me.
4. I am increasingly aware of everybody and everything around me.
5. I am aware of the existence of God.
6. I know God's plan for me is to share His infinite Universe.
7. I welcome change and challenges as. God's indication to me for my need to grow into new and higher understanding.

Affirmations for Developing Self-Control

1. I am in control.
2. There is no habit nor behavior stronger than the power of my mind.
3. I have full and complete control and dominion over my senses and faculties at all levels of my mind, including the outer conscious and inner subconscious levels.
4. I have the control to practice self-discipline as a way of life.
5. With the help of God, I am developing the power I need to maintain the control needed to improve my life.

Affirmations for Developing Self-Discipline

1. I achieve control through self-discipline.
2. Self-discipline is good for my body, mind, and soul.
3. Self-discipline makes me strong and ready to do God's work.

Meditation

Meditation is a technique whereby you voluntarily lower your brain wave frequencies to an altered state of consciousness while maintaining awareness. When you achieve the so-called meditative state, your physical body is in a state of relaxation. Although your mind is also relaxed, it has reached a higher level of awareness, through which your spirit has achieved a higher state of consciousness.

While you are existing within the body, your mind is the key to entering higher levels of awareness and consciousness. When you are at these higher levels, you can achieve mastery over your body and emotions.

The important aspect of meditation is that it is voluntary and under your complete control. It is your decision and responsibility when and how to use it.

Certain forms of meditation become mental exercises. Just as when we physically exercise, our muscles develop and maintain strength, active meditation helps us develop our mental abilities and powers. The more we employ meditation, the better our mind power and the closer our goal becomes. On the other hand, when we stop meditating, our mental powers will deteriorate just as our muscles do when we stop exercising.

Active meditation is when we actively form images while we are still and quiet in the meditative state. In my opinion, passive meditation has little or no part in PAT.

Technique. Although it is not impossible to learn to meditate from a book, personal instruction is far superior. Employing cassette tapes may be a reasonable alternative. Individuals who desire to solve serious health or personal challenges and children and young adults with pre-existing problems probably require serious personal instruction.

If you wish to try it on your own, try the following technique:
1. Find a quiet place, sit in a comfortable chair, feet flat on the floor (legs not crossed), hands on your lap, and with your head positioned so that it lies along the center of gravity of your spine.
2. Close your eyes and take several deep breaths and exhale slowly, trying to use your diaphragm for breathing (this may take practice to get used to).
3. As you exhale each breath, tell yourself that your body is going to relax from head to toe.
4. You may wish to count slowly from ten to one or see yourself in an elevator on the tenth floor slowly descending to the first. As you count downward to one or the elevator descends to the first floor, envision your muscles relaxed, starting from your scalp to the tips of your toes.
5. Continue taking deep breaths and exhale slowly.
6. As you arrive at the count of one or the first floor, say to yourself: "My body is relaxed. My mind is relaxed. I am relaxed. Although my body and mind are relaxed, my mind is alert, sharp, and active."
7. Then begin to repeat slowly affirmations you wish to impress upon yourself or play a cassette tape containing the affirmations you wish to program.
8. Or perform guided imagery which is described below.

9. **Caution:** Try not to fall asleep which defeats the whole purpose of meditation. You need to be in the meditative state with awareness for best results. Techniques to remain conscious during meditation are described in the *Manual of Positive Attitude Training (PAT) Techniques.* Try to stay in meditation 15 minutes or longer. When working with children, continue for at least 30 to 45 minutes each evening. They will get used to the time. It can be a practice in self-discipline.

Guided Imagery

Guided imagery is a technique whereby, while you are in the meditative state, you create and visualize with your imagination situations or conditions as you want them to be. Your subconscious self then brings them about.

This is actually how the mind functions normally. Although we are not usually aware of it, our hidden imagination feeds the subconscious with ideas and pictures with which to function. Some conditions are good. Others are not so good. This is why we must be aware of what we are creating as thought forms, so that the subconscious is at all times presented with ideas and pictures which we consciously desire.

Behind many of our mental and physical disabilities are our negative creative imaginings. We allow our subconscious to be fed such things as fear, hatred, jealousy, limitation, failure, etc. when we energize gossip and bad stories, and recycle bad news. The subconscious is constantly drawing from the memory bank for the raw materials to create our everyday reactions, feelings, and emotions.

We create these negative creative imaginings for

our children to experience. Then, we wonder why they develop poor self-images or feelings of little self-worth. Whatever parents harbor as thought is psychically conveyed to their children. So it would be wise for parents to do their homework and insure that their children develop strong positive uplifting psyches.

We practice guided imagery during meditation because it is at the altered states of consciousness, at the slower, stronger brain wave frequencies of ALPHA and THETA, that we get the mental power to make stronger impressions on our brain cells, enhancing the storage of these positive creative imaginings within our memory bank.

This is the technique you can use to see yourself handling and mastering situations in life. Teach children to visualize themselves paying attention in school, reciting their studies from memory, having great powers of concentration, and being more creative. Teach them to relax if they are hyperactive, or to visualize themselves with a dry bed in the morning if they are bedwetters.

If children (or anyone else, for that matter) can sucessfully visualize an event repeatedly in meditation, the event becomes a reality in their lives. Spaced repetition of any kind builds belief. Need I repeat: **belief creates reality.**

Technique: When you wish to teach children how to relax, ask them to:
1. Enter the meditative state and picture yourself lying on a beach on a beautiful summer day, or lying by a forest stream listening to the trickle of the brook with a slight breeze blowing through the trees overhead, or walking through a forest on a beautiful fall day with the sun shining through the trees with their reddish-golden leaves.

2. Create any situation that is peaceful to you and get absorbed by the beauty of this imaginary world you've created or which has appeared.
3. Experience your cells and mind relaxing.
4. Experience your spirit leaping into another dimension.

Give your children sufficient time to do these exercises. Perform the exercises with them.

When you wish to help them solve a particular health challenge, ask them to enter the meditative state and ask them to picture themselves normal and well. Ask them to openly describe what they are experiencing while they are meditating with their eyes closed.

When your children are experiencing difficulty in school, possibly in relating with a teacher or their peers or getting poor grades, ask them to visualize themselves accomplishing what they desire.

Teach them to use guided imagery to picture themselves handling life's situations as they would like them. Help them to practice being aware of and to monitor their thoughts. Help them create positive thoughts. Teach them to take hold of the reins. They **can** learn to move or change their course according to their desires. Assist them in writing out their goals so that crystallization will occur.

What children create in their imaginations at these strong brain wave levels is what they will eventually experience in life. What they can accomplish with guided imagery depends upon their belief and how much they work at it.

Summary

Mental functions improve with practice. Through the use of mental games, children can learn how to develop positive attitudes. This is the basis of PAT. Affirmation is one of the key ways of convincing the subconscious that you mean business and of developing a positive belief factor. Meditation is the technique whereby you voluntarily lower your brain wave frequencies to an altered state of consciousness while maintaining awareness. In this state you can tap your inner mental powers to transform your desires into reality. Guided imagery is a technique whereby, while you are in the meditative state, you create and visualize with your imagination situations as you want them to be. This process helps to crystallize thoughts and ideas into reality.

The garden worker

Creating a vision of a garden is not enough. Before a crop can ever be harvested, laborers need to do much work in the fields. Constant vigilance needs to be maintained to insure that the plans of the architect are carried out. Laborers are needed to continue the watering, weeding, pruning, etc.

The chief laborer within the garden of each individual's life is the individual him/herself. Early in the spring of life, children need to learn that they are primarily responsible for the growth of their own life-force. Their instruction needs to be watered with encouragement to implement and activate their learnings and to persist in cultivating their crops of self-responsibility, self-awareness, self-control, and self-discipline.

CHAPTER 6

THE HOME ENVIRONMENT

The next three chapters deal with particular problems and challenges facing children in their three major environments, namely, the home, school, and play. Although it may be somewhat artificial to deal with these separately, it is easier to write about them thusly. The reader is nevertheless advised that these three environments intermesh in a child's life as one world and have to be considered so in real life.

Conception to birth

One might consider that a child need not be concerned about the world prior to birth. I hope to convince you differently.

We've heard stand-up comics make jokes about children selecting parents or children angrily retorting to their parents that they did not ask to be born and not to blame them (the kids) for being born. Ah! An interesting concept of children selecting parents! Would they have made a better choice? Or would they have blundered as many parents feel they have done? Some individuals strongly believe that a spirit prior to incarnation through birth has some influence in selecting parents. I don't intend to open that Pandora's box nor do I have an opinion about the matter!

There are some important factors to consider during the period of an infant's existence as an embryo, then as a fetus.

The fetus might ask, "Are these prospective parents of mine ready for me? Did they plan for me or am I some mistake? Will I have two parents or one? Will I know who my father is? Are my parents children themselves, either by age, mentality, or both? Am I going to be reared by grandparents who are too old and tired to care or who did not plan for me either?"

The fetus might ask; "What is my mother smoking, cigarettes or pot (cough . . . cough)? What is she eating? What is she doing to her lungs? What is she doing to her brain? What is she doing to **my** brain? What kind of chemicals is she taking into her body that are affecting me and also affecting her ability to care for me after I'm born? She doesn't seem to care now. Will she care after? Is that my father smoking, too? Will he be alive when I graduate from college . . . from high school?"

The fetus might ask, "What kind of environment am I being born into? They already have two small brats; can they do better with me? Are my parents ready for me? Dear God, do I have a choice?"

It is the responsibility of parents to be ready for children. Is the home environment conducive to the additional long-term assignment of raising children? This is no game. It is the responsibility of parents not only to provide for the physical needs of their children, but also for their mental, emotional, psychological, and spiritual. It is an awesome responsibility which should be taken seriously. Parents can hope to learn more when the actual experience is happening — true; however, there is still much that can be done to pave the way beforehand by way of attitudes to equip parents and their offspring for a wholesome life. It is the responsibility of parents to insure that their children are equipped to face life with positive uplifting attitudes rather than in fear, hatred, failure, or any other negative experience.

It is time during the period from conception to birth of the child, or even sooner, for parents to learn what they hope their children will learn from them. **Children learn by example,** and, dear parents, it begins right now!

The first year

The child is born. "Isn't she cute? Uh-oh, the baby's crying? Her diaper's not wet or dirty. She must be hungry. But I just fed her. Oh, I'll give her a bottle anyway."

Now that I've mentioned it, what about diet? Are we parents really careful about what we feed our babies? The dietary habits of the individual are starting now. In this country, as it is in almost the whole western world, we still tend to overfeed our infants and children. Then we wonder why they are fat at six months, at one year, at 16, as adults. Earlier we talked about habit prevention as habit control. Let us be mindful of what, how much, and how often we feed them at this time. Start applying the principles described in Chapter 10.

Are you a relaxed parent, or are you nervous, uptight, and fearful? Newborn infants can psychically sense the emotional vibrations close to them and will respond accordingly. **Nervous parents beget nervous children. Relaxed parents beget relaxed children.** As a parent, become aware of your assets and liabilities. Improve your assets and diminish your liabilities. If you wish to teach your children how to increase their awareness of themselves, shouldn't you also develop self-awareness? You **can** do it. You can do anything you desire. God has given you everything you need to be a complete person. Nothing is missing, and you know God is still around to help you. All you need to do is ask.

Do you fight in front of your infant? By the way, did your parents fight in front of you . . .? Bad habit! Start now to demonstrate love around your child and watch the love reflected back to you from the infant.

Do you wish your child to develop patience, understanding, tolerance, joy, love and all those other beautiful positive emotions? Then you as a parent must practice them now. Make it a habit in your life and your children will develop similar habits in their lives.

Can you spoil an infant? Yes, **you can spoil a child at any age.** Experienced pediatricians frequently can detect a so-called **spoiled** child very early, sometimes as early as the first month of life. At least, one can observe the distinct personality developing which has a good chance of running into trouble later. When I started practing pediatrics, I used to inform parents of my opinion that their child was developing a tendency to become "spoiled." I usually did this when I felt sure, sometimes after three months of age and older into adolescence. I then learned that parents do not like to be told of possible aberrations in their children's personalities and many of them transferred to other physicians. I then went through a period when I said nothing about it. I did not feel comfortable with this stance. So I then approached it by saying, "I feel your child is exhibiting a tendency toward being spoiled. Of course, I might well be wrong. You as a parent are a better judge of the situation then I. Since I am the child's pediatrician, I feel duty bound to share my concerns. After all, that's what you pay me to do. If anytime in the future you might agree and wish to discuss it in more detail, please let me know. The earlier you correct behavior problems the better and easier they are to correct."

Invariably I was **totally** ignored! But, at least, they didn't transfer to another physician! I felt that I had done my duty. The lesson was that most parents become masterful at denial.

The story doesn't end here. As I observed these children, their behavior worsened and their parents literally fell apart at the seams little by little, taking tranquilizers to cope, some resorting to drinking, others physically abusing their children. And, still the denial continued.

Many, when their children reached 4 or 5 years of age, would return, some crying, reminding me of what I had said 3 to 4 years previously, and asking, "Is it too late to do something now to correct the situation? Can anything be done?" My reply, "Of course there can. Let's see what we can do together."

The message to parents is simple. Become involved in raising your children. Be aware of your children's needs, their behavior, etc. Do not assume the attitude that it "will not happen with my children." Measures to correct or change anything can start only when recognition and willingness to accept the situation takes place.

Preventive measures are even better. Continue the practice of developing the positive attitudes you started during pregnancy. Start to teach your children by affirmation and example to do the same. As a parent, become aware of your attitudes because they cannot be hidden. Take a stand in every area of your life — **BE** that which you want to experience. Do whatever it takes to get there, and **as one practices, one develops, then demonstrates.**

The child during the first year of life is developing psychodynamically and the first ideas, thought forms, and events are so very important. They are being stored in memory for future use. If you desire to give your children a legacy, consider a living legacy they can use the rest of their lives — a computer filled with positive attitudes.

Ages one to five

These are the early exploring years for children. They begin to venture beyond the crib and explore all those beautiful breakable household items! It might also appear to the child that those parents of mine are always in **my** way. During this time there are many potential exposures to negativity.

"Don't touch that. Get away from there. No, you don't do that. No, you can't go there. No. No. No. No." Some of the first language a toddler hears is negative. And what is one of the first words parents hear reflected back to them? What is the first word most children really are convinced they know? You guessed it. It's "no."

An important point to realize is that the mind cannot process a negative. If you ask someone not to think of a banana, for instance, the process of saying the word "banana" creates the picture within the mind, the very picture you asked not be created.

When you ask or tell a child not to do or touch something, in the process of doing so you have created the picture you wished the child not to think about. The solution would be to divert the child's mind to something else you would rather he do. Approach your child and ask: "Why not play with this? Let us do this. Come, help Mommy do this." Begin to use your imagination as a parent to be creative in handling your children. It will pay enormous dividends.

As children explore outside the home they begin to interact with non-family members. They develop friends. If you think raising children was a challenge before, it becomes more so now. Your child begins to get exposed to other households whose values may be different from yours. Peer pressure begins to exert its influence upon your child and it continues to grow, reaching an enormous peak at adolescence. What's a mother to do?

Insist on your right to be the parents of your children. Other parents can do what they wish with theirs, but insist they do what you want with yours. If you decide that it is unhealthy for your child to eat sweets, soft drinks, and junk foods, then Johnny's mother next door is not allowed to feed **your** child those items under any circumstances. This also applies for grandparents. If you allow your child to be exposed to situations you believe are detrimental to his growth and development and ignore it, you are giving tacit approval to it. Your child gets confused and begins to wonder about all the other things you've been telling him.

Good example and consistency must be the rule in rearing children. Something should be said at this point about **rigidity.** Rigidity implies uncomprising inflexibility and, like its opposite, is relative depending upon an individual's attitude. In my opinion, the best guide to determine rigidity is the aware person. Develop increasing self-awareness and an open mind. To eliminate rigidity, practice letting go of old concepts that do not fit into your life now. If you think you are being too rigid, become flexible and back off. Admittedly, one of the challenges in life is to be firm but not rigid. Rigidity or inflexibility places tremendous burdens upon your inner self. Rigid people nearly always seem to be looking for something to be upset about. Try to teach your children to be firm but kind with their inner self and to be flexible with life, accepting change as indicative of the Universe's vital nature.

Ages six to eleven

The early school experience is next in a child's development and we will explore these years from its effect within the home.

Children are spending more time outside the home environment, usually about six hours a day. That is almost half of their waking hours during the week. They must learn to deal with other major authority figures (i.e., teachers and principals) for the first time. They are being exposed to values, many of which are different from what their parents presented to them. Children get caught between parents who think they are right and teachers who are just as adamant that they are the professionals and parents don't know anything anyway. This experience can become a challenge of enormous proportion for the child.

Children also begin to discover the element of peer pressure. If they have little self-value and weak personalities, they may succumb to foolish dares to raise their image or to feel good about themselves. They are increasing their circle of friends and they are beginning to place a value on friendships. They may begin to compromise their principles in fear of being considered different. The pre-adolescent years from 9 to 11 are psychodynamically challenging. During these years sexuality is beginning. The sex hormones are increasing and the so-called *end organs* are responding. Children desire privacy and a whole new realm of interpersonal friendships and relationships develop. Usually boys hang around with other boys and girls with girls in their quest to satisfy the new-found curiosity of this age group. This is a far cry from what is in store for them (and their parents) in the ensuing adolescent years!

Children are beginning during these years to make independent decisions, many of which they do not share with their parents. They are learning that there are consequences attached to some of the things they do. Their taste of independence outside the home is brought into the home environment and parents must deal with this.

As children develop this new-found wisdom, they begin to question their parents about their ways and why does it have to be their way all the time. Parents begin to realize that their influence is shaky. No one warned them about this. Of course, no one told them it was going to be easy either!

First, parents, stay cool! If you have instilled positive attitudes into your children, they will be able to recognize and accept positive events and reject negative situations. If you have trained your children to be creative in their thinking, expect to be challenged. It will all be for the good. Offer to discuss openly **all** situations, but reserve the right to pull rank if you deem it necessary. Your children will have their turn when they become parents. Continue using PAT in youself and your children to reinforce the systems of values. By now you should realize that it has to be a way of life in order to work.

If parents have not done their homework till now, they may wish to institute PAT at this point, the earlier the better.

Twelve to seventeen

The adolescent years are upon not only the child but also the parents who soon learn that their own adolescence was considerably easier to handle than their children's! The reader might react when I occasionally attempt to present situations with tongue-in-cheek humor. It is worthwhile to digress for a moment to explore the role of humor in raising children.

No one ever said that raising children shouldn't be fun. Even though this is serious business, it can still be humorous. In my opinion it must have humor. For without humor parents may never get beyond their children's adolescent years!

Lack of humor and enthusiasm is a kind of sour attitude that breeds stress. A humorless person is generally one who is seething inside and full of self-reproach and self-contemptl

Learn to be humorous. Use humor not only when things look great, but also when things seem stressful or when times get tough. Those around us will lighten up also. Teach your children humor. Learn to extract the fun out of life. Teach your children to do the same.

If you've thought that being a parent up until now was like walking a tightrope, you haven't experienced your children's adolescence. The ground rules are all changed. The games are different and no one bothered to explain the rules or give you the gamecard!

During adolescence young adults also begin to value and to become concerned about their own identities and they resent any encroachment. Parents need to learn to respect their teenagers' privacy and learn to trust them and not just give lip service to this trust. Tune into this channel and open the door for them to express what is going on inside of themselves — their feelings, especially. An understanding attitude breeds a basis for a trusting relationship to exist.

Parents cannot abandon their teenager who is still somewhat immature (although he or she would never admit it). Parents still have the responsibility to guide their teenage children, even at times when they may not want the guidance.

Also characteristic of adolescents, particularly during the latter half, is the experience of thinking they are in love. This may occur at least several times as a preliminary to the eventual choice of a marital partner. Try to recall what you wanted at this critical time in your life to make it easier or bearable.

A problem frequently arises about teenage friends of whom you as a parent do not approve. Before judging the situation, learn all you can about your teenager's friends. Try to look beyond the physical appearances of shabby clothes and long hair and find out what they are thinking about, where their minds are.

Be as supportive as you can possibly be. If you disagree about some friends, meditate with your child and pray for mutual understanding. If you still believe you are right about the possible bad influence of a particular friend or *crowd,* express your feelings and explain your reasons, then allow the situation to turn without resistance on your part. Frequently, what one resists, persists. Occasionally, if everything else fails, you may have to move swiftly and do what you must to sever a relationship.

There is such a thing as psychic energy. You can be affected by the people with whom you surround yourself, and you in turn can affect them. If you surround yourself with negative individuals and losers, unless you are aware of how to detach yourself, you will be affected negatively and your chances of also becoming a loser are great. On the other hand, surrounding yourself with uplifting, positive individuals, winning and creative people will result in your becoming a positive, creative winner.

The same applies for children and teenagers. The best we can do as parents is to guide them to the highest levels of consciousness of which they are capable. The friends with whom they surround themselves will influence their growth. If they realize this, fine and well. If they don't, they will soon learn.

As adolescents master the biologic, psychologic and cultural challenges of this stage of development, they once again draw closer to their parents. Ultimately, they take their normal place in society as cooperative, constructive, and hopefully creative young adults. Be particularly careful not to create new problems which will tend to interfere with the adolescent's so-called return to the fold. Adolescence is both an exciting and challenging stage for both the teenager and parent. Fortunately, the stormy aspects *blow over.* The sea is calm again.

PAT instituted early in life will lessen or eliminate many adolescent hang-ups. Because of the teenager's determination to establish his own identity and the potential ability to resist parental authority and fight back, the problems of this period are better prevented than treated. For this reason prepare your children early in life so that their attitudes can have a head-start in dealing with the vicissitudes of life, positively and creatively.

Eighteen to twenty

This is the period of legal independence. We are including a brief discussion of these years because young adults at this time still respect parental opinions and require parental guidance and assistance. Many young adults continue their education at universities and need financial, moral, and psychological support from parents. Some are challenged by their continued dependency upon their parents and they will eventually realize that average parents take great joy in giving to their children, something young adults soon realize when **they** have children of their own.

The young adult during these years is ready to assume greater responsibility over his own life and within the home government, especially if he is still living at home. Parents want their children to gain in independence and continue developing their leadership abilities which, by the way, have been going on since early youth, consonant with their increasing maturity.

The young adult may be out in the work force and needs to learn how to deal with supervisors and perhaps with subordinates if he is a supervisor himself.

PAT started early in life and continuing now can prepare the young adult to become a wholesome, cheerful, and creative moving force, able to influence others to regard the art of living similarly. As a parent, your doors are always open for a creative input into your children's lives. Your reward will be the satisfaction that your efforts produced healthy fruit — your offspring.

Postscript

This chapter was not meant to be a compendium of details on the psychological development of children. Rather, it deals with some of the factors affecting the way children think as they grow to maturity. This chapter is meant to stimulate authority figures to become aware of their subjects so that potential problems can be pinpointed and dealt with before they become heavy-duty challenges. However, even if one finds that the problem is full-blown, all is not lost. Implementing PAT at any stage of the game will produce improvement over the situation. PAT is a way of establishing positive, uplifting, creative attitudes within the minds of children and young adults. Achieving this will prepare them for experiencing life more abundantly.

The winter-early spring garden environment

In the winter the garden is far from dormant. The soil is undergoing the great and important process of renewal. Dead plants from the previous growing season are being reincorporated into the soil and transformed into basic nutrients for the plants of the upcoming season. The hard winter destroys the weak perennials and portions of trees and bushes, and the surviving plants are strengthened. In the spring, additional nutrients are added and the soil is tilled so that all the food and air is mixed. The soil is renewed and ready to receive the new seeds. The quality of growth in the garden is a result of this silent process of renewal.

Similarly, the home environment provides the working *soil for the development of the child. It is important for prospective and present parents to provide the best soil and environment in the home so that the child's roots may be firmly established and well nourished. This involves reverence and respect for life, commitments to quality nurture and proper preparation before birth and at all stages after birth.*

CHAPTER 7

THE SCHOOL ENVIRONMENT AND STUDY HABITS

Introduction

Beginning at about age 5 or 6, children spend almost half of their waking hours during weekdays for about 10 months of each year in school. If we were to consider school-related work and events (e.g., homework, special projects, activities, etc.), this time would significantly increase to well over 50 to 60 percent.

How do children and young adults view this school experience, this new environment outside the home? What effect does school have upon their future development into adults? What new challenges must they face that they were not exposed to at home?

This chapter attempts to answer these questions and to discuss the overall psychodynamic influence going to school has upon the child.

The responsibilities of teachers and the overall school system in educating children and training them to use their minds for self-development are discussed in Chapter 14.

Kindergarten

Kindergarten usually serves as a transition experience between full time in the protective home environment and serious school business. Although most children welcome and enjoy kindergarten, some are not ready for it and become frightened at the loss of parental presence and at the new relationships with strangers to which they are exposed.

In my opinion, kindergarten is almost a useless and costly adventure and the money used to support it could better be spent for real education. I would propose that children be eligible to attend the first grade between the ages of 5 to 7. At this stage of development, chronological age is not necessarily the best criterion upon which to base the decision about beginning school. Degree of mental and psychological maturity would be a far better measure. If a 5-year old child were ready, he would be able to enter the first grade. If a 6-year old child were not, he would be allowed to wait an additional year until he is 7, by which time all children must be enrolled. The purpose of this book is not to defend my personal bias, but rather to suggest ways of teaching children how to develop positive attitudes and prevent problems of psychological maladjustment. A further description and explanation of the psychological dilemma kindergarten creates will be found in Chapter 14.

Nevertheless, children must at one time or another face this new school environment. It is their first serious exposure to surrogate authority outside the home. Other temporary authority figures (e.g., babysitters) usually were in their home, an environment the child has already learned to manipulate skillfully. School, however, is different.

School is where the child is also exposed to so many strange faces and unknown personalities. The child may need extra help to learn to accept this challenge and deal with it to succeed.

Children during this period develop new fantasies about themselves and their world. Many of these fantasies are **real** to children at this age and verbalizing these fantasies to their parents sometimes creates another challenge: the fantasy which may be real to the child is unreal fantasy to the parent. These situations may involve teachers, friends, and other peers. Try to relate to the child's expression and support his imaginative quest — make a game out of it — but ultimately with a feeling that the child is O.K.

First to sixth grade

During this period children undergo continuing, gradual biologic maturation of the central nervous system, permitting increasingly skillful and coordinated physical maneuvers and advancing intellectual capacity.

Children are being challenged increasingly by their peers and teachers to perform physically and intellectually. Challenges usually arise with the so-called *slow* child who may withdraw into himself when he feels he cannot compete successfully with his peers. His assessment of self-worth and his self-esteem diminish to the point where he begins to see himself as a failure. This may appear as learning disabilities such as dyslexia and poor memory, and the development of these situations further hamper his success and aggravate his deteriorating self-image.

Instead of withdrawing, the *slow* child may become aggressive and belligerent both to his teachers and to some of his peers. He becomes the *bully.* He is attempting to compensate for a diminishing feeling of self-worth by convincing others, and especially himself, that he is strong, overpowering, and in control of the whole world. What he cannot accomplish with his academic record and achievements, he is attempting to achieve by his behavior. But it doesn't work. When this happens, an understanding attitude may be the first step in rooting out the cause and reversing the behavior pattern.

We have had children in our T-H-E-M-E Positive Attitude Training Camps who attended because of failing grades and hostile behavior in school. Our assessments were that they suffered from intense inferiority complexes. Their self-esteem was at low levels and required rebuilding. During the PAT camp experience they learned how to relax, how to view their peers and authority figures with respect and without fear, how to visualize themselves as achieving good grades in school, and how to see themselves as winners instead of losers. They learned how to believe in themselves. Since **belief creates reality,** they became winners! One 13-year old child was hostile and failing most of his subjects. Within the year following the PAT camp experience, he became one of the top children in the Gifted and Talented program in his school district.

Problems also frequently arise with the exceptionally bright children who find themselves not being stimulated and challenged enough. Many of these get bored, cannot sit still in school, become *acting out* problems for the teachers, and are eventually labeled as "hyperactive." Physicians are consulted and many of these children are placed on *dexedrine* or *ritalin* — they are **drugged** to make them manageable in the school system (Chapter 14).

During these school years, children may develop an identification with a teacher of the same sex as a model for identification. They may idolize a teacher but at the same time keep that teacher under very close scrutiny, an awesome responsibility for the idol.

Children may form or get involved with clubs, usually with members of the same sex, as they create a kind of society of their own making and fantasies. The clubs with boys may take on qualities of *gangs* if the aggressive feelings and destructive fantasies get out of hand. In these times of women's liberation, *female* school gangs are becoming commonplace.

There is an increasing interest in sex identity and in their own sexual powers as they approach preadolescence. This may involve a more serious exploration of themselves or of teasing their peers, both of similar and opposite sexes. This may be further strengthened or aggravated by gang involvements.

As children further refine their physical and intellectual abilities, their ego strength develops. They begin to challenge everyone, including most of all parents, who are no longer viewed as all-knowing and all-powerful figures. Children increase their skills in manipulating both authority figures (parents and teachers) and peers.

Very important during this period, children are learning a trait common to adults, suppression and denial of important knowledge about self. True self-awareness turns into confusion.

Seventh to ninth grade

This may be an artifical category but with the increasing development of middle schools it may develop into a significant school group with the psychodynamics of the preadolescent, pre-high schooler.

This, of course, is another transition period for children, leaving the child-world behind and looking forward to the grown-up world of high school.

Children are beginning to explore the opposite sex in a semi-play/serious fashion. Toward the end of this period, children face puberty and all its physical and psychological ramifications.

They begin to identify with older peers who replace teachers as idols. Coincident with this, but not necessarily the result of, preadolescents begin their exposure and experimentation with drugs (e.g., marijuana, "speed," and other more dangerous substances), a frustrating situation for all concerned: teachers, principals, parents, and young adults.

Tenth to twelfth grade

This period essentially coincides with puberty and adolescence. There occurs a sharp rise in the rate of body growth, an increase in size of the gential organs, change in body configuration, development of secondary sexual characteristics, and the appearance of menstruation in the female and ejaculation in the male. More aggressive behavior is exhibited towards members of the opposite sex and sexual games with peers and older individuals increase. Not only are teachers vulnerable to these games, students are influenced by their teachers' covert or overt sexual actions and behavior. Fantasies take on a whole new meaning and dimension.

During this period students develop the capacity for the highest form of abstract thinking and reasoning, a real challenge for the teacher. Students begin to question the meaning of everything, and their queries might stump the best philosophers.

Learning disabilities are usually ignored as management of behavior and aggressive problems becomes a major concern for the teacher. Students are at the peak of their ability to rationalize everything, usually a subtle form of denial. When grades fail, they begin to divert themselves away from purely academic pursuits.

Feelings of internal disorganization and inadequacy are denied and covered up by bravado and loudness. Unpredictability and impulsiveness become ways of controlling drives and feelings.

Identity with peer group is approaching the highest level it will ever achieve in an individual's lifetime. This will diminish abruptly upon graduation from high school as each teenager moves toward independence and begins to concern himself with his role in adult society.

Whenever untoward behavior appears to repeat itself in a child, let this be a sign that special attention is in order. Employ a compassionate approach in an attempt to understand what the real matter of concern is. Children are more apt to cooperate with a person who is sincerely and kindly motivated.

Summary

The school environment is the child's first serious exposure to surrogate authority outside the home. The child learns to deal with other personalities (some friendly, others not) and succeed. Children are being challenged increasingly by their peers and teachers to perform physically and by their teacher for intellectual advancement. Mental and study habits developed during the school years continue through adult life. Adolescence is an especially trying time as children attempt to balance academic pursuits and peer pressure. Toward the end of high school, students are developing the capacity for the highest form of abstract thinking and reasoning as they prepare themselves for a role in adult society.

The late spring environment

Another aspect of the spring activity is to provide conditions necessary for individual plant development. One job might be to thin the carrots and lettuce so that each of the remaining plants has sufficient room to grow. Hoeing and mounding of the soil help support the growing plants. Plants are helped to survive the early struggle for independent growth and development so that by summertime they can mature to adult plants. Interaction between plants then begins to occur in preparation for cross pollination and breeding. Plants grow straight or crooked, depending upon how they react to the rigors of wind and rain.

In the garden of life, children's minds and bodies are cultivated by teachers in school, where they are prepared for maturity and adulthood. Interaction with other children provides exposure to new ideas, life styles, and habits through which the child can grow straight or crooked.

CHAPTER 8

THE PLAY ENVIRONMENT

Introduction

In the early stages of this book's conception as I meditated on the topics to include, I was inspired to include a chapter on "The Play Environment." Initially I did not understand the reason or significance of such a topic and on one occasion I was about to scratch it from the Table of Contents. But I did not. I felt compelled to meditate some more. The results are now obvious to all: the topic and chapter remained.

We live by the games we play. Our minds function according to the mental pictures we create. And our lives are either enhanced or diminished depending upon whether our games (or attitudes) are positive or negative. The life games we learn to play as children we continue to play as young adults and then as supposedly mature adults.

The mind does not distinguish between a picture created in play or one which is serious. It recognizes **only** the picture and proceeds to act accordingly. Some believe that God (or the Universe, whichever you feel comfortable with) is totally supportive and cooperative to **all** of your ideas. It will say "yes" to your positive creations; it will say "yes" to your negative thoughts. You and only you are responsible for everything that happens to you. The mind can be trained by the playing of **mental games.** In fact, this is the way the mind normally operates. In PAT we employ games to "get the picture."

Let us explore some aspects of play, how it can affect our thinking, some of the pitfalls of negative game playing, and suggestions on how to transform the play environment into a useful growth and development experience.

Harmful games adults play with children

Children learn almost everything initially from adults. Some of the games adults play with children involve getting children to submit by **scare** and **fear** tactics. How many times does a mother threaten her child by saying, "Wait till Daddy comes home," rather than disciplining the child herself at a time when the child can make a mental connection between the event and the punishment? And then, the mother wonders why the child fears her father.

I would like to have a dollar for every time I have overheard a mother in my office threaten her child by saying, "If you don't listen to me, the doctor will give you a needle." And then she wonders why her child fears doctors.

How often have parents threatened their children by saying, "The police will come and take you to jail." Then, children learn to fear rather than respect policemen.

The mind is more influenced by what it sees than what it hears. A threat is translated into an image and both get recorded in memory and the child fears the picture he has created within his own mind, the vivid fantasy, of his father coming home to beat him, of the doctor jabbing him with that "humongous" needle, the policeman putting him in a dungeon and throwing the key away.

The sad reality is that, once stored, the pictures remain within the deep recesses of the child's subconscious. They may surface from time to time as bad scary dreams which represent another negative picture which also gets stored, building the pile of subconscious negativity.

If children are taught fear they grow up becoming fearful.

Games children play can tell you something

Observe your children playing their imaginary games either with dolls, toys, or just play-acting in their rooms. What they say and do can tell you where they are in their fantasy world.

When they play house, are they cruel with their imaginary children or are they lovable? Do they punish them severely and beat them to a pulp? Are they reflecting what they are observing from their parents or some of the "sick" puppet shows they observe on TV?

As a parent are you amused by the cruelty of your little children, or by their fears, or by their anger in their play situations? (Be amused no longer.)

Do your children call their imaginary (or real) playmates "dummy," "stupid," "fool?" Do you call your children these names? What children do in play reflects what they have been exposed to through their parents, other individuals, TV, comic books, etc., and it reflects how they are beginning to see their world.

If children play out hostility and anger in their fantasies, they harbor hostile and angry thoughts within.

On the other hand, if children play games of joy and love, they harbor thoughts of joy and love within their hearts and minds.

Fantasies

I have already mentioned fantasies several times throughout this book. Question: are fantasies really fantasies to a child? I would like to propose the provocative answer, "No!" Let me explain.

Thoughts are real. They represent energy and they have actually been photographed. Kirlian photographes taken of plain water has little or no aura. Kirlian photographs taken of the same water after a priest has blessed it has a huge aura. Kirlian photography is a process whereby the object to be photographed is placed in a special electrical field while being exposed to the film (see *The Kirlian Aura: Photographing the Galaxies of Life,* Stanley Krippner and Daniel Rubin, Editors.) What is the difference between the unblessed and blessed water? The blessed water has absorbed the positive thoughts placed there by the priest. Numerous experiments performed with psychic healers give evidence of the fact that thoughts are forms of energy and as such are real.

Consider any material object, such as the table I'm using to write this manuscript. This table would not exist had it not first been conceived within the mind of an individual. So the table represents the physical manifestation of what once existed in another realm as mental thought energy. The table can be described as an example of **positive creative imagining.**

Fantasies are thoughts and as such are real to the mind and what is real to the mind represents reality. **Belief creates reality.** If children fantasize that they are winners, they **are** winners and in time this will be manifested in the physical realm. On the other hand, if in their fantasies children see themselves as fearful and as losers, they are full of fear and **are** losers. In time this will also be manifested in the physical realm.

Have you ever had the opportunity to interview successful individuals? Ask them about their fantasies as children. Invariably they saw themselves as successful back in time as early as they can remember. They had faith in themselves. They crystallized this faith with work, and hence the physical reality of a successful individual.

As children repeat their fantasies they give more energy until their thoughts are crystallized into physical reality. The reader may have noticed that I use the term *physical reality*. I do so because the term *reality* is ambiguous. There are *physical, mental,* and *spiritual* realities and it is important to modify the word *reality* by indicating which realm it is in. Figure 8-1 depicts the energy spectrum and the various levels (or realms) of reality.

Learn about your children's fantasies. They may indicate areas that could be helped by PAT.

Dreams

Reverend Batzler discusses the significance of dreams as a spiritual tool for self-discovery. My purpose here is to discuss briefly another aspect

THE REALMS OF REALITY

	Physical	Mental	Spiritual
Relativity	$E = mc^2$ (death)	→	$m = \dfrac{E}{C^2}$ (creation)
Example of laws	Gravity	Mental Cause – Physical Effect	Genuine miracles: a phenomenon which apparently defies physical/mental laws. Law of 10-fold return; Reap what one sows; Karma. Readiness: when the pupil is ready, the master appears.
Energy	Crude: low level	Refined: higher level	Ultimate: highest levels
Time/space dimensions	Time–Space finite	↔	No time / No space infinity
Radiation spectrum	Spectrum of electromagnetic radiations from 1/10,000 Angstroms (beyond nuclear reactors on the one end) to 100,000,000 meters (beyond 60 cycles AC on the other end).		Unknown

Figure 8-1

THE PLAY ENVIRONMENT 113

of dreams as a tool indicating what is stored within the biocomputer and how we can use dreams to tell us what we need to correct in our minds.

Dreams are like fantasies in that they tell us what children are thinking. An important aspect is that dreams are pictures coming from deep within the subconscious mind.

The average individual dreams every 90 minutes of sleep and there can be numerous dreams each evening or one continuous dream which is picked up when each REM cycle returns.

Individuals who claim they do not dream still process through this automatic cycle. However, they do not recall the events. Remembering dreams can be an important tool in learning about oneself, as they indicate what is within our subconscious mind through its symbolic language.

One does not necessarily have to know why a particular dream occurs in order to correct it. I was counseling a 45-year old woman who was probably the most fearful person I had ever encountered. Her body was as rigid as concrete and she was tense from within out. She was unable to work longer than two consecutive days without staying home to rest on the third day. Since she used up her annual and sick leave as it accumulated, she had to take numerous days as "leave without pay."

Since about age 10, this lady would go to bed each evening, sleep about 30 minutes, have a frightful dream of monsters and the "angel of death," wake up full of fear and scared, and pace the floor for about an hour. She would go back to sleep and the same pattern would be repeated over and over again. In the morning she was physically, mentally, and spiritually exhausted. She constantly cried. She felt that she was bad and God was punishing her for something she might have done as a child. She didn't even know what it might be.

She was scheduled to take our T-H-E-M-E Training Seminar for Adults one weekend but postponed it to go to a workshop where someone was going to teach body-mind attunement through physical movement. I had hoped that entering this other experience with a positive attitude might help her.

However, on Wednesday of the following week, she telephoned me in tears. She said that the weekend helped her while she was undergoing the experience, but by Monday her symptoms of fear and rigidity were returning and by Wednesday, the day she called she was back to her old miserable self. I asked about her dreams. She said they were the same and had been for the past 30 years.

I indicated to her that it was my opinion that her rigid body and fearful emotions were expressions of her thinking, and that during the workshop experience she was able to relax her body by the physical techniques taught and applied, but that after it was over, her rigid, fearful subconscious thoughts caused her body to be re-transformed into a hunk of concrete. (She walked around like a piece of concrete with legs!) I told her there was a purpose for her dreams — they tell her what is going on within her mind, her belief system — and that she should try to correct the situation that has existed within her mind for 30 years.

She did undergo T-H-E-M-E training. One month later I saw her. She was happy and "loose as a goose" as she put it. I asked her about her dreams. She replied that now she dreams only of angels and beautiful spirits. She has recently written me. Her handwriting had considerably improved over what it had been before. She continues to be relaxed, full of energy, and happy. Her willingness to give up the old concepts about herself, through PAT, transformed her life.

PAT does work and you can observe the effects this training has upon dreams which are deep subconscious events.

Movies and TV

As previously mentioned numerous times, the mind believes more what it sees than what enters through any of the other senses. Individuals think they can be amused by watching negative movies and TV. Let's consider the impact of some of these.

Recently, the movie industry has produced a rash of scary movies. After the success of *Jaws,* the movie industry decided to give the public what it wanted. The movie *Jaws* broke **all** box office records up until that time, far surpassing *Gone with the Wind,* which had been for years the unsurpassed leader. Individuals who view *Jaws* are seeing people being ripped to pieces by a man-eating shark. Blood and fear are pictured with all the realism Hollywood has at is disposal. These fearful pictures enter the subconscious mind and get stored as bits of information. Later these bits of information are used by the mind to create other confusing and fearful events which can be expressed as inability to cope with normal everyday challenges, fear of uncertainty, indecision, etc. They may influence an individual's dreams to further perpetuate fear and uncertainty.

Following *Jaws,* the movie industry produced such films as *Towering Inferno, Jaws II, Airport I,*

II and *III, Earthquake,* etc. These are examples of **negative creative imaginings.** These pictures are destructive and interfere with one's ability to sustain positive, uplifting attitudes of fearlessness, inner strength, joy, etc.

Many of the average TV shows are no different. They depict life and situations contrary to a wholesome existence. They are created by individuals who desire to entertain, to become successful by making money, and are not really focusing on (and probably care little about) how minds are being influenced by them.

The TV news is another culprit of reinforcement. A friend of mine was an Army major in charge of security for one of the most prominent American newscasters who headed a team doing a documentary on the Viet Nam War. The prominent newsman never left the plush surroundings of his hotel. Every evening he and his team would review the films of the day to select what they would use for their documentary. Any film which had the slightest evidence of representing anything positive was discarded. The prominent newsman would select the goriest depictions of the war and say, "Oh! I like that. That's a **good** one," and so on. Eventually the documentary represented the judgement, the **negative creative imaginings,** of a single man who, by the way, is almost revered among newsmen and the public at large.

Individuals watch TV news, become depressed, and their whole lives begin to fall apart at the seams. The inability to cope with stress and stress-related illness is becoming the major disease epidemic the world has ever known.

Let us protect our children from this legacy by teaching them to develop positive attitudes and to reject the negative creative imaginings of other people.

How to transform games and play into useful realities

This book is concerned with children and young adults. We have already discussed how to observe children to determine what kind of imaginary games they play and what is in their fantasies and dreams. PAT techniques can help children transform fantasies and dreams into meaningful events. When these are positive, they actually are reflecting a positive inner subconscious.

Monitor the movies and TV programs your children watch, especially the younger ones. There are many good movies and TV programs which are entertaining and/or educational.

Use positive mental games to teach your children how to develop their self-worth and self-esteem, how to see themselves as winners and leaders, and how to view themselves as kind, understanding and tolerant of their parents, peers, teachers, subordinates, etc.

Let life be an enjoyable experience, full of fun and games. Life is our play environment. Let us teach our children to experience the *joy of living* by creating their *joy in life*.

Play in the garden

The garden is not all work. There is also play. Bees and birds play with the plants and blossoms, pollinating them and ridding the garden of harmful insects. Rain falls freely on the parched sod and the sunbeams dance with the shadows. The gentle breeze plays soft melodies on the leaves.

In life, children grow through play which includes imagination, fantasies, and dreams. When these are positive, genius blossoms — if negative, genius does not emerge.

CHAPTER 9

EFFECT OF MEDICINES AND OTHER DRUGS ON ATTITUDES

General aspects

We have within ourselves a built-in system of checks and balances which operates to keep the body and mind functioning properly. This is called *homeostasis,* which is defined as the tendency to maintain normal, internal stability in the organism by coordinated responses of the organ systems that automatically compensate for environmental and internal changes. This system is so finely tuned that interference usually results in harm to the body.

There are systems which increase our heart rate and blood pressure to accommodate the increased needs of our muscles when we are physically exerting ourselves and exercising. There are systems that cause increased blood flow to the skin to help us lose heat in the summertime and to decrease blood flow to conserve heat when we are cold. When we eat, the body shifts blood away from the muscles and to the intestinal "portal" circulation to help in digestion and assimilation of foods. In the bright sunlight the pupils of our eyes constrict and in the dark they dilate so as to allow the correct amount of light for us to see. There are many more homeostatic control mechanisms working all the time, to which we give no thought at all, thanks to our subconscious.

We have known for many years the damaging effects such drugs as morphine, hashish, marijuana, LSD, etc., have upon our ability to perform physical and mental functions.

We are now beginning to realize that the use of tranquilizers and other so-called *legitimate* drugs (we call them legitimate because they are prescribed by physicians!) interferes with our body's internal mechanism to control normal body functions. Additionally, they alter our mental, emotional, and spiritual attitudes and interfere with our ability to deal with normal challenges of life and stress. *Tranquilizers which are supposed to help you deal with stress actually work against our built-in system designed to help us deal with stress.*

This chapter describes some of the bad effects drugs (both illegal and legitimate) have upon the ability of children and young adults to develop positive attitudes about life and upon the body's mechanisms to handle some physical dis-ease states. Drugs alter the chemistry of the brain and **interefere** with functionings of the mind.

The reader is referred to an earlier book, *How to Benefit from Stress,* by the same authors, 1979, Hidden Valley Press. Chapter 9 in that book deals with *The Destructive Tranquilizers* and covers some points and illustrations not mentioned here.

Physical damage caused by drugs

The suppression of natural defense and treatment mechanisms. Tranquilizers and other psychotropic drugs are powerful chemicals which interfere with brain chemistry. We now know that the body makes substances called *endorphins*. These *endorphins* are chemically indistinguishable from narcotic drugs such as morphine. Now, I ask you, "What is the body doing making morphine-like drugs?"

Well, it appears that we have an internal mechanism to control pain. When we need to mobilize it, we can cause our own body to produce these narcotic-like *endorphins* which go to the site of an injury or dis-ease and relieve pain. They are produced in many areas within the body, both within the central nervous system of the brain and spinal cord and in areas associated with peripheral nerves. These substances enter the blood stream and arrive at the site of action where they must attach to specific receptors. In fact, this is how they were discovered. Researchers performing investigations on how morphine works within the body discovered specific receptors for morphine. They wondered why the body contained receptors specific for morphine, a drug extracted from the poppy pod. Did God in all His wisdom create these sites so that when man discovered morphine this drug could work? Probably not. So the researchers suspected that the body produced its own morphine-like substances to accommodate the specific receptors. Amazing deduction! And it is true.

Once the receptors are full, it may take a day or so to regenerate the receptors again so that the *endorphins* can attach and work again. This is the reason why after several days of administering morphine derivatives to a patient with chronic pain the drug doesn't work as well for a time. This is also the reason why acupuncture goes through a refractory period when it doesn't work in a patient with chronic pain.

Exciting research is now being done to investigate how the release of these **naturally** occurring pain control substances can be triggered by deep massage, acupuncture, acupressure, meditation, biofeedback, etc.

Isn't it interesting that we have within our body a mechanism to produce pain-killing substances. We also have the ability to release these substances when we need them by using the power of **our** mind through concentration and meditation. What more would we want? Does anyone really need morphine and other pain-killing drugs? Do you need them? Do your children need them?

It is also interesting that we have built-in mechanisms to produce other substances, those related to *endorphins,* which affect our moods and our ability to cope. The release of these substances is also internally controlled.

We are a chemical factory and our body functions as a result of biochemical reactions. Our minds depend upon the brain which functions as a result of complex bioelectrochemical reactions. The *endorphin* system worked long before researchers discovered it. What other vital chemicals do we have the ability to create within our own body to help us function physically, mentally, emotionally, and spiritually?

Taking drugs such as Valium, Darvon, and other psychotropic and tranquilizing drugs interferes with the body's intrinsic mechanism to relieve pain and deal with emotional challenges. Darvon, for instance, has a morphine-like chemical structure. It attaches to the specific receptors without relieving pain. It does, however, block the *endorphins* from attaching, thus preventing the internal system from working.

Tranquilizers, sedatives, and narcotic drugs can mask important symptoms of serious disease. Larry was 16 years old when I first met him. He had been on Valium for one year to control attacks of hyperventilation. His mother had attended a workshop I presented on "The Role of Body, Mind, and Spirit in Holistic Healing." She was concerned about her son being on Valium. She asked me whether I could cure her son, using meditation. I told her I could not, but that Larry could if he learned how to meditate and apply himself toward this goal. Larry came and attended the T-H-E-M-E Training Seminar for adults. We attempted during the week of the seminar to wean Larry from his Valium.

Larry had been to his family physician who made the diagnosis of hyperventilation after being told by his nurse who had seen one of Larry's attacks that it was hyperventilation. Larry was given a paper bag and instructed to breathe into it when he felt an attack coming on, a commonly-accepted method of treatment. He was then sent to a neurologist who performed an EEG and some other tests and concluded that there wasn't anything he could do to help. Larry was then sent to a pediatric psychiatrist who prescribed Valium which definitely lessened the severity of the attacks.

On the last day of the T-H-E-M-E Training Seminar, Larry was doing fine although he informed me that he had had one of his attacks. That evening he had a longer one. When his mother described the event, I began to have questions about the diagnosis being correct. I was not his physician and had no reason to question the diagnosis which I knew had been confirmed by both a neurologist and a psychiatrist. Two days later, Larry was still experiencing his hyperventilation attacks. I suggested that his mother allow Larry to come to my home where I could teach her son more specific imagery and possibly have the opportunity to observe one of these attacks. Larry came one evening and during supper had a most peculiar attack — something I had never seen before. (I thought perhaps I missed reading a page in one of the medical textbooks at Harvard!) I wasn't sure what it was, but I knew what it was not. It was not hyperventilation. Within 30 minutes after his first attack in my home, Larry had what appeared to be a *grand-mal* generalized convulsion. Again it was the most peculiar convulsion I had ever seen. Larry was asked to employ mental imagery to control these attacks which occurred almost every 20 minutes while he was awake. He was able to control every one of them after that by employing imagery. This, however, was not getting to the cause.

The following morning, I admitted Larry to the hospital, performed more tests, and concluded that Larry had a brain tumor, the symptoms of which had been successfully **suppressed** by Valium while his tumor grew larger and larger. He underwent a successful operation, the tumor was removed, and Larry subsequently did well.

There is one very important difference between using your internal mechanisms to control symptoms of dis-ease and employing medicines and drugs. The former works along with other internal stabilizing forces. Drugs may work against such homeostatic mechanisms. Let me explain.

Larry was able with meditation to control his convulsions. If he were able to check and possibly destroy the tumor by mobilizing his internal immune system, his symptoms would have disappeared completely. This was not attempted because of the advanced nature of the tumor and its location in a vital area of the brain. He would **not** have been able to completely control the seizure symptoms by meditation while the tumor continued to grow. The body's innate wisdom overrides any other internal regulating mechanism that may interfere with vital elements. Meditation and positive imagery are safe.

The use of drugs, on the other hand, is not. Tranquilizers, such as Valium, narcotic pain killers, and others drugs can override key body warning mechanisms. This was the case with Larry. The Valium did control his seizures (warning symptoms of serious dis-ease in this case) while allowing the tumor to grow. It was indeed fortunate that Larry had a mother who was not satisfied that her son had to take Valium indefinitely.

The suppression of physical strength. If you ever have the opportunity, read a package insert (an information sheet supplied by manufacturers about a drug) to see what is written about *Contraindications, Warnings, Precautions, and Adverse Reactions* of specific tranquilizers and sedative drugs. If your doctor or pharmacist will not show one of these to you, peruse a copy of the P.D.R. *(Physicians' Desk Reference)* which you can find in most bookstores nowadays. You will notice that from 80 to 90 percent of the printed information is devoted to harmful effects and side reactions of these drugs.

Most of the package inserts and ads warn of drowsiness, confusion, reduced physical capabilities and depressed menal alertness. Those who are depressed take tranquilizers to elevate their moods. They may achieve this. One of the prices they pay is suppression of their physical strength and vigor. Can you imagine the mind being totally convinced that you feel fine when your body feels all **zonked** out? I will discuss in Chapter 11 how important exercise is to develop a feeling of physical well-being to convince the mind that you are well. So why take drugs which interfere with this?

Children taking psychotropic drugs are affected also. They too experience reduced physical strength and vigor. Children should be taught how to be mentally alert and maintain physical vitality. A happy child is one who is constantly on the move. Such activity is a result of an elevated mood which in turn can be reinforced by vigorous physical activity. Each feeds the other in a positive way.

Addiction

Tranquilizers, sedatives, and narcotic drugs are addictive. Much of the advertising of these drugs states that with usual dosages the problem of addiction does not occur. **This is false.** Addiction almost always occurs after long-term use of about 3 to 4 weeks. The degree of addiction, however, is usually dose-related.

For instance, if you were to take 2 to 5 milligrams of Valium 2 to 4 times per day for 3 weeks, and then decide to stop taking the drug, you may experience agitation, probably more so than when you started. You have actually become dependent upon the drug. You are using the drug as a crutch rather than facing up to the real challenges of life. Upon withdrawal, you may experience difficulty sleeping, find it hard to concentrate, and become irritated at little things that did not bother you before. (Your family may even notice it and suggest you take your Valium!)

If you were to take up to 50 to 60 milligrams of Valium per day and stopped abruptly, epileptic seizures would probably ensue. This type of withdrawal symptom indicates severe addiction and is the type recognized by physicians and drug abuse centers. It is dramatic. This type of withdrawal requires hospitalization as in the case of someone coming off *hard* drugs.

The central nervous system gets used to drugs and eventually becomes **dependent** on them.

All drugs are addictive — it is only the degree of addiction that varies. Young adults who smoke *pot (marijuana),* take LSD or PCP *(angel dust), uppers* and *downers,* etc., are becoming addicted to these drugs. Eventually, a price will have to be paid for this addiction.

Suppression of mental and natural creative abilities

Tranquilizers and other psychotropic drugs also suppress mental activity and natural mechanisms which deal with emotion. You don't have to believe me. Read a package insert for one of these drugs and see what the manufacturers say about their own compounds.

All psychotropic drugs (illegal and prescription) interfere with attention, concentration, and memory — three very important mental functions. Mental confusion can also result. Learning can be severely affected. Is this what we want for our children?

Psychotropic drugs alter our dreams so that attempt at interpretation is useless. If your subconscious is talking to you through the dream mechanism, why garble the message? It makes no sense. Tranquilizers and sedatives interfere with the normal 90-minute cycle of brain wave activity and suppress REM sleep, the most regenerative sleep state. Dreams are interrupted, garbled, or suppressed entirely.

Other psychotropic drugs such as LSD and PCP can cause you to have hallucinatory dreams and hallucinations during the waking state. The deleterious effects of these chemicals may persist for months and years after cessation of the drug. Permanent brain damage has been observed.

In my opinion, psychotropic drugs alter and interfere with LB/RB balance and interfere with creative thinking. A young man once remarked that LSD caused him to be more creative: he could develop all sorts of pictures in his mind he could not create before. He felt creative because he felt he had the power to fly. When he said this, I knew I had him. I answered him by asking him several questions. Of what use are these pictures to him if they do not represent some creative reality? Of what use was the feeling that one could fly to those individuals who attempted the feat and crashed dead to the ground? Of what use is a thought, if it is not reconciled with the physical reality at the time? Of what use is a chemcial which is known to alter one's brain chemistry to the point of making one a hopeless imbecile?

The hyperactive child

Special mention is being made here of those children branded as being hyperactive and/or having a poor attention span. It is almost a crime to administer psychotropic drugs, such as dexedrine and ritalin, to those children without first accessing their true mental capabilities.

We have had experience with these children in our PAT camps. They can gradually be taken off these harmful drugs, placed on a sensible diet (Chapter 10), and taught how to relax and be creative. The average so-called hyperactive child has an above average I.Q., which is hard to reconcile with his poor performance record in school. More about this in Chapter 14. Important are the facts that these children have high mental activity, they can learn to channel this energy in creative pursuits, they can be happy and productive in life, and they do not need chemical drugs to suppress all of this and further destroy their self-image.

Conclusion

Our ability to create images, ideas, and thoughts is the most precious gift we have. Taking chemicals which would interfere with this God-given talent is downright stupid. We have been given control over our body, mind, and spirit. We must rally to this charge by being responsible, and developing awareness and control through discipline.

Let us be concerned about these things as we teach our children and young adults, as we learn together, how to *awaken the genius* within, and to get the most out of life and be happy and responsive to our Creator while doing it.

PAT is designed to teach children how to turn on and control these fantastic chemicals we have within our body, to function holistically, that is, with body, mind, and spirit unified.

How to control the weeds

Seeds of other plants, most of which are weeds, find their way into the garden. These weeds need to be eliminated before they choke out the productive plants. The gardener can either selectively and carefully pluck out the weeds, leaving the good plants to grow, or apply a chemical weed-killer to do the job. The former is a natural way and doesn't introduce harmful chemicals which are absorbed by the good plants and transmitted to the fruit. The choice of which method to employ depends upon the gardener.

What about the weeds in our lives? Do we take chemicals (drugs and tranquilizers) to suppress the negative emotions and to make us better able to withstand the stresses of life? Or do we go within and uproot the unwanted weeds and give space and energy to the positive plants which grow, blossom, and bring forth the fruits of good thoughts, words, and deeds?

CHAPTER 10

EFFECTS OF DIET

Introduction

The food we eat affects the quality of life itself. Most individuals would admit that diet relates to the health of our physical body. However, the fact is also true that it influences our thinking, emotional responses, and even our spiritual health. The basis of holistic health is to bring the three aspects of man's nature — body, mind, and spirit — into harmony, so that we function as a whole person, rather than as three separate schizophrenic entities working against each other.

This chapter relates to diet as it affects mental functions, expecially in children. The reader is again referred to our earlier book *How to Benefit from Stress* (1979, Hidden Valley Press) for a more complete discussion on diet and how it affects physical, mental, and emotional health states. That chapter in the previous volume is even more applicable to children and young adults because many of the dietary indiscretions contributing to dis-ease states take years to cause harmful effects. Much physical illness can be prevented through dietary sanity.

Effects of diet on mental and emotional health

Diet affects the quality of our everyday life, how we feel, how we think. Many of the foods we are exposed to are contaminated with herbicides and pesticides, most of which are **neurochemical paralyzers**. With the advent of *no-till* farming, a substantial increase in the use of chemicals was required to control weed growth and pests.

Many foods contain naturally occurring chemicals which affect the central nervous system. Caffeine (in coffee, tea, chocolate, and cola) and alcohol are discussed below in more detail. Ingesting too much of these foods will alter our neurochemistry and affect our thinking.

Other chemicals are added to our foods to retard spoilage *(preservatives)*, to make them more pleasing to the eye *(artificial colors)*, or to enhance the way foods taste *(artificial flavors)*. These also affect behavior, especially of children, who appear considerably more sensitive to the effects of these substances, probably because their metabolism is clipping along at a faster rate than adults.

Diet affects our emotional responses. If you have a tendency toward depression, go ahead, take a shot of alcohol and see how depressed you can really get. If you have a tendency toward being hyperactive and have jittery nerves, go ahead, continue to drink stimulating drinks such as coffee and cola and continue to eat refined sugar; observe how much more nervous you'll become.

Are you quick to anger, are you aggressive, and do you devour other people, bringing their wrath down upon you? Continue to eat red meat and watch how your aggressive behavior continues.

Diet affects the way children think, and the way

they think affects their ability to cope with stressful challenges. Allowing them to eat foods and drink beverages which make them nervous, irritable, grouchy, and unpleasant will affect their behavior at home and in school.

Diet is the most important factor in keeping your child's physical body healthy. When the body is ill, the mind soon becomes ill, then the emotions become affected. The reverse is also true. When the mind is ill, the emotions are affected. Eventually, the body develops dis-ease.

Parents don't need to be told this. We knew it all along. We parents remember how our children acted the last time they had even as minor an illness as a simple head cold. We easily recall what happened to their physical strength and vitality. We even remember how it affected their emotions and thinking.

Effects on concentration, learning, and memory

Hyperactive children are the extreme examples of how diet affects concentration, learning, and memory. They are the epitome of the learning disabled.

Dr. Ben F. Feingold *(Why Your Child Is Hyperactive*, 1975, Random House, New York), an allergist, was the first to suggest that hyperactivity was caused by allergies to food additives. His now-famous diet eliminates food colors, dyes, additives, and salicylates.

Other researchers have not completely confirmed Dr. Feingold's conclusions, probably because he did not eliminate sugar and other potent food allergens. A more recent study demonstrates that the following foods are implicated as causes of hyperactivity: *(in decreasing order of importance)* **sugar; food colors, additives, flavors and dyes, especially red food coloring;** caffeine-containing drinks and foods, such as **coffee, tea, chocolate,** and cola; **milk** and milk products, such as cheese and ice cream; **citrus** fruits and drinks; eggs; nuts and peanuts; potatoes; soy; beef; pork; apples; chicken and grapes. **Sugar is by far the greatest dietary culprit causing hyperactivity in children and nervousness in adults.**

An allergy to any food can cause a child to be hyperactive. It is impractical to eliminate all the foods mentioned at the same time. However, it would be prudent to first eliminate the major culprits listed in bold type. This would result in curing most hyperactive children. Those very few who are not helped will require additional dietary investigation.

This section deals with foods and substances which affect not only concentration, learning and memory, but also behavior of children. At the outset it is highly recommended that the following toxic foods be either eliminated or avoided, especially if you have children who are having these difficulties. Other toxic foods which do not appear to affect behavior but which do affect overall health are described in Chapter 10 of *How to Benefit from Stress.*

Toxic foods

Refined sugar. All parents interested in their own health and in the health of their children, should read William Dufty's book, *Sugar Blues.*

Refined sugar has been implicated in many disease states, including hypoglycemia, diabetes, tooth decay, cardiovascular dis-ease, and many psycho-emotional conditions.

Hypoglycemia, low blood sugar, is a very common problem afflicting individuals today and it is directly related to increased intake of refined sugar. This condition causes children to experience weakness, headaches, and even convulsions in the severe state. A misconception of many is that low blood sugar should be treated by ingesting more sugar. In fact, the opposite is true: eating sugar only temporarily raises blood sugar. This is followed by a rapid drop in blood sugar, especially in the individual prone to hypoglycemia attacks.

Hypoglycemia is actually a misnomer. The correct term to use is *hyperinsulinism.* Individuals with this condition are very sensitive to rapid rises in blood sugar. Their systems react by releasing too much insulin which, in turn, drives the blood sugar down again, usually to levels below those before the sugar was ingested. The treatment for such a condition is to eat protein and complex carbohydrates which results in a slow increase in blood sugar. In this situation the body does not react with a tremendous outpouring of insulin. Rather it is slowly released and a more even level of blood sugar is maintained. Sugar is to be avoided **completely.**

Children prone to wide variations in their blood sugar have difficulty concentrating, paying attention, and sitting still, especially when their blood sugar drops to low levels.

In addition, sugar increases the metabolic rate and keeps the system on a *high.* This works against attempts to relax and enter the high energy meditative brain wave states. Taking children off refined sugar and significantly decreasing their intake of natural sugar concentrates such as honey is a **must** in hyperactive children and others experiencing difficulty concentrating and being attentive in school or at home.

The average Westerner eats 120 pounds of refined sugar per year, or almost 25% of the total calories. The U.S. public consumes 11 million tons of sugar per year. The increased use of sugar is traceable in large part to the desire of food manufacturers to create unique food products with a competitive edge: for example, Nabisco's Oreo cookie with double the amount of sugar filling, and the addition of sugar to cereal in 1948 to recover slumping cereal sales. Today, we find sugar not only in cold cereals, baked goods, and snack foods, but also in such foods as canned vegetables, canned fish, baby foods, soups, and even in prepared meats such as bologna, hot dogs, etc. The tremendous increase in sugar usage is directly related to refined sugar being added to processed foods. The U.S. Department of Agriculture's 1971 figures show that 70% of the sugar we consume is in food products and beverages — not directly under the control of the consumer, although the consumer always has the choice of not buying nor eating them.

Like salt, the desire for sugar is not a physiological necessity but an acquired taste. Dr. Yudkin (ref., *Dietary Goals for the United States)* found that sugar consumption not only causes an increase in blood-sugar levels, but also results in a sharp rise in adrenalin, the "fight-or-flight" hormone, which may explain why sugar gives such a rush in energy, or such a fidgety feeling. **Sugar addiction**, and an addiction is what it is, may have its origin in the biochemistry of this hormonal joyride. **This effect is particularly worse when sugar is fed to children.**

Many individuals are unaware of the actual amount of sugar they either consume themselves or allow their children to eat. The data shown in Table 10-1 may shock many to appreciate this reality and stimulate them to correct their bad dietary habits concerning sugar consumption.

In *Dietary Goals for the United States,* The U. S. Senate's Select Committee on Nutrition and Human Needs recommends that sugar consumption be reduced by about 40% to account for about 15% of total energy intake. We at The GOTACH Center believe this is even far too much, especially for children who are developing their food cravings and addictions which will last them a lifetime. Refined sugar has **absolutely** no reason to be in the diets of children, or of adults for that matter. It does no good. In fact, it causes ill health conditions. Eliminate refined sugar completely from your children's diet, insure that their grandparents and your friends and the parents of your children's friends do not feed sugar to **your** child. Learn to enjoy the benefits of natural carbohydrates and sugar substances.

Cola and other stimulating drinks. Substances which allegedly overstimulate the brain, central nervous system, and mind will cause children to be nervous and uptight. High on the list of such chemicals is caffeine.

Coffee, which contains the highest amount of caffeine, is, of course, the greatest culprit for adults — one cup of coffee has 90 to 125 milligrams (mg). Coffee is also consumed by many children and young adults. A cup of tea contains 30 to 70 mg.

Have you ever wondered how much caffeine is found in various soft drinks consumed by chil-

Table 10-1
Refined Sugar Hidden in Popular Foods

Food Item	Size Portion	Approximate Sugar Content in Teaspoonful of Granulated Sugar*
Beverages		
cola drinks	1 (6 oz bottle or glass)	3½
cordials	1 (¾ oz glass)	1½
ginger ale	6 oz	5
highball	1 (6 oz glass)	2½
orangeade	1 (8 oz glass)	5
root beer	1 (10 oz bottle)	4½
Seven-up®	1 (6 oz bottle or glass)	3¾
soda pop	1 (8 oz bottle)	5
sweet cider	1 cup	6
whiskey sour	1 (3 oz glass)	1½
Cakes and Cookies		
angel food	1 (4 oz piece)	7
apple sauce cake	1 (4 oz piece)	5½
banana cake	1 (2 oz piece)	2
cheese cake	1 (4 oz piece)	2
choc. cake (plain)	1 (4 oz piece)	6
choc. cake (iced)	1 (4 oz piece)	10
coffee cake	1 (4 oz piece)	4½
cup cake (iced)	1	6
fruit cake	1 (4 oz piece)	5
jelly roll	1 (2 oz piece)	2½
orange cake	1 (4 oz piece)	4
pound cake	1 (4 oz piece)	5
sponge cake	1 (1 oz piece)	2
strawberry shortcake	1 serving	4
brownies (unfrosted)	1 (¾ oz)	3
chocolate cookies	1	1½
Fig Newtons®	1	5
gingersnaps	1	3
macaroons	1	6
nut cookies	1	1½
oatmeal cookies	1	2
sugar cookies	1	1½
chocolate eclair	1	7
cream puff	1	2
donut (plain)	1	3
donut (glazed)	1	6
snail	1 (4 oz piece)	4½
Candies		
average choc. milk bar	1 (1½ oz)	2½
chewing gum	1 stick	½
chocolate cream	1 piece	2
butterscotch chew	1 piece	1
chocolate mints	1 piece	2
fudge	1 oz square	4½
gumdrop	1	2
hard candy	4 oz	20
Lifesavers®	1	⅓
peanut brittle	1 oz	3½
Canned Fruits and Juices		
canned apricots	4 halves and 1 T syrup	3½
canned fruit juices (sweet)	½ cup	2
canned peaches	2 halves and 1 T syrup	3½
fruit salad	½ cup	3½
fruit syrup	2 T	2½
stewed fruits	½ cup	2

*Approximate amounts of refined sugar (**added sugar, in addition to the sugar naturally present**) hidden in popular foods.
**Actual sugar content.

Table 10-1
Refined Sugar Hidden in Popular Foods

Food Item	Size Portion	Approximate Sugar Content in Teaspoonful in Granulated Sugar*
Dairy Products		
ice cream	⅓ pt (3½ oz)	3½
ice cream cone	1	3½
ice cream soda	1	5
ice cream sundae	1	7
malted milk shake	1 (10 oz glass)	5
Jams and Jellies		
apple butter	1 T	1
jelly	1 T	4-6
orange marmalade	1 T	4-6
peach butter	1 T	1
strawberry jam	1 T	4
Desserts, Miscellaneous		
apple cobbler	½ cup	3
blueberry cobbler	½ cup	3
custard	½ cup	2
french pastry	1 (4 oz piece)	5
fruit gelatin	½ cup	4½
apple pie	1 slice (average)	7
apricot pie	1 slice	7
berry pie	1 slice	10
butterscotch pie	1 slice	4
cherry pie	1 slice	10
cream pie	1 slice	4
lemon pie	1 slice	7
mince meat pie	1 slice	4
peach pie	1 slice	7
prune pie	1 slice	6
pumpkin pie	1 slice	5
rhubarb pie	1 slice	4
banana pudding	½ cup	2
bread pudding	½ cup	1½
chocolate pudding	½ cup	4
cornstarch pudding	½ cup	2½
date pudding	½ cup	7
fig pudding	½ cup	7
Grapenut® pudding	½ cup	2
plum pudding	½ cup	4
rice pudding	½ cup	5
tapioca pudding	½ cup	3
berry tart	1 cup	10
blancmange	½ cup	5
brown Betty	½ cup	3
plain pastry	1 (4 oz piece)	3
sherbet	½ cup	9
Syrups, Sugars and Icings		
brown sugar	1 T	**3
chocolate icing	1 oz	5
chocolate sauce	1 T	3½
corn syrup	1 T	**3
granulated sugar	1 T	**3
honey	1 T	**3
Karo® syrup	1 T	**3
maple syrup	1 T	**5
molasses	1 T	**3½
white icing	1 oz	**5

*Approximate amounts of refined sugar (**added sugar, in addition to the sugar naturally present**) hidden in popular foods.
**Actual sugar content.

dren? Recent studies reveal the following: Coca-Cola, 64.7 mg; Dr. Pepper, 54.2 mg; Tab, 49.4 mg; Pepsi, 43.1 mg; RC Cola, 33.7 mg; Diet RC, 33 mg; Diet Rite, 31.7 mg. Most parents who wouldn't give their children coffee because of the caffeine think nothing of allowing them to drink soft drinks in amounts containing **more** caffeine than the average adult consumes from coffee and tea.

This may account for a child who is cranky, hard to please, has a behavior problem or may be experiencing difficulty in concentrating, having learning problems, or who is hyperactive. If your child has difficulty sleeping or is a bedwetter, these behaviors can also be related to caffeine.

I'm always asked, "What about decaffeinated coffee?" That's probably worse! Decaffeinated coffee might seem like a reasonable alternative for coffee lovers who want to avoid caffeine. Unfortunately, there are two health hazards as consequences.

First, the chemical solvent that almost every decaffeinating process employs today to leach the caffeine from the green coffee beans is *methylenechloride.* This substance, which is in the same chemical family of *chlorinated hydrocarbons* as dry-cleaning fluids, is currently under suspicion as a potent cancer-inducing agent. The National Cancer Institute is currently investigating the effects of inhaling and ingesting methylenechloride. However, the results of these tests are not yet available. In the meantime, the FDA has placed a maximum level of permissible solvent residue in roasted decaffeinated beans at 10 parts per million, a figure many sources still consider risky. Second, the decaffeinating process introduces an amount of nickel that many consider toxic and dangerous.

There is a lesson here: **chemical alteration of foods usually results in chemical residuals which in themselves may increase the toxicity of food.**

Teach your children not to develop the habit of drinking coffee, tea (except herb teas), cola-containing and other soft drinks. You will notice the calming effect which eliminating these drinks from their diet will have. Teach them good health habits now so that they may enjoy living.

Chemical food additives. The effects of chemical food additives upon the hyperactive child are now generally well-known and appreciated.

Modern technology is responsible for the production of tremendous quantities of food to feed the population masses. Never before in history have we had the know-how and capability of virtually eliminating hunger from the world. The author questions the wisdom of how this technology is being applied. More than ever, industry is using chemical food additives, such as colors, flavors, preservatives, thickeners and other substances, for controlling the physical properties of food. There are more than 1,300 food additives currently approved for use in the U.S., and the exact amounts being used are unknown.

The Food and Drug Administration in 1976 estimated that the **average daily consumption of artificial colors alone among children aged one to five may be about 75 milligrams.** The largest single category contributing to artificial coloring consumption among children is beverages. More accurate measures may be available after the FDA completes its 1977 survey.

The FDA bases its consideration of the safety of chemical food additives upon varying degrees of testing, review of scientific literature, expert opinion and long-time usage. Most of the testing has involved animal toxicity studies with artificial colors. Artificial flavors have been tested the least. In 1977, the FDA began a re-evaluation of the safety of colors, flavors and direct additives.

What information can animal studies provide? The varying degrees and quality of animal testing may provide useful data on the effects of chemical additives on the animal systems employed, but how can these results be related to man? Our life span is approaching three-quarters of a century and the effects of chemical additives consumed as a child might not become evident for 20 to 60 years.

There are continuing discoveries of apparent connections between certain additives and cancer. Some definitely have been implicated as causative agents in hyperactivity. This gives justifiable cause to seek to reduce additive consumption to the greatest degree possible. There are increasing numbers of knowledgeable and concerned scientists in this field who advocate that only those additives that serve a necessary function should be permitted in food. What is necessary is defined as that which is needed to insure food safety.

Ruth Fremes and Zak Sabru in their publication *Nutri Score* have classified as unnecessary and possibly a hazard to health several additives commonly considered under the heading of preservatives and flavor enhancers, e.g., nitrates and nitrites, BHT, BHA, and monosodium glutamate. Referring to nitrates and nitrites, *Nutri Score* comments:

> While these additives are not in themselves harmful, they may combine with other chemicals in food or in the intestines to form nitrosamines, which are

known to cause cancer. The advantage of using nitrites in processed foods is that they maintain a pinkish-red color, which makes the meat look fresh and attractive, and they check the growth of bacteria. Some of these bacteria, like botulinum, produce deadly poisons. Government should therefore limit the addition of nitrites to the amount needed to check growth of botulinum bacteria and no more.

This has been done in Canada, where the Canadian Health Protection Branch has recently reduced the amounts of nitrates and nitrites allowed in cured and processed meats. Industry, for its part, should find a preservative other than nitrite that will be effective against bacteria, yet will not present a cancer hazard. (Quoted from *Dietary Goals for the United States,* February 1977 issue, page 56.)

The chemical preservatives BHT and BHA are not essential and there are foods on the market not employing these additives.

There is even less need for the chemical monosodium glutamate, (e.g., Accent), which is merely a flavor enhancer and not a necessary food additive. This chemical has been associated with headaches, flushes in the head and body, and tingling in the spine. (It, by the way, is also a source of sodium and can be hazardous to individuals who must restrict their sodium intake.)

Let us analyze for a moment the reasons why certain additives are employed. **Artificial colors** are employed solely to make the food pleasing to the eye. Have you wondered why so many soft drinks are colored red? It's because red emits stimulating vibrations, thus increasing the desire to drink more. The bright yellow color of butter and margarine, the deep blue color of some soft drinks, the bright colors of cake frostings, etc., are all psychologically geared to get your attention and to excite you into desiring that food. Children are particularly vulnerable to this psychology.

Motivation for eating and drinking should be hunger and thirst and nothing else. In my opinion, the single most important factor contributing to physical dis-ease in our society today is that we eat too much. Obesity seriously contributes to a child's deteriorating self-esteem. Enhancing the color of food solely for the purpose of enticing us to eat more is against all principles of good health. The practice of adding chemical coloring agents should be stopped.

Artificial flavors are used to enhance the way food tastes or to impart a flavor where there is little natural flavor. As we use more flavorings we suppress our taste buds. This is what happens when we constantly use salt. The same is true when we use sugar, sugar, and more sugar. In fact, sugar is now being used by food manufacturers to accommodate the "sweet tooth" of the U.S. consumer. As mentioned earlier, sugar can now be found in the most unsuspecting foods, such as canned vegetables, canned fish, baby foods, soups, and even prepared meats such as bologna, hot dogs, etc.

Fortunately, the suppressive effect added flavoring has upon the taste buds is reversible. Returning to a diet rich in native grains and vegetables with some canned fish can enhance our tasting ability to the point where natural foods become enjoyable and pleasing to eat.

Artificial preservatives are employed to prevent spoilage and destroy harmful bacteria. Remember that *preservatives are poisons and anti-metabolites,* that is, they destroy basic living enzyme systems. Is this what we want our children to take into their bodies?

There are some natural methods of preserving which do not add poisons to the body. These include salting, pickling in brine, drying, freezing, refrigerating, etc. There are many foods, such as whole grains, root crops, etc., which can keep for long periods of time without spoilage, provided there are proper conditions.

We must be on our guard not to introduce into our bodies industrial chemicals that our cells are unable to deal with. As we become more aware of how chemicals affect our body, we will then be more careful about what we consume.

Be alert. Begin reading labels. Become an educated consumer in the market place. Learn to prepare meals *from scratch* using natural unprocessed basic foodstuffs. Let us protect our body and our children's bodies from the chemical onslaught. Our health and life, and theirs too, may depend on it.

How allergy affects various dis-ease conditions and behavior in children

To appreciate how allergy may result in various dis-ease and behavior states, it would be worthwhile to appreciate what occurs in an allergic reaction. When an allergen (a substance foreign to the body) is introduced into the system, the body responds by developing antibodies — special proteins which combine with allergens to neutralize and eliminate them from the body. Some antibodies are of the *good* type, and others are not so good. When these latter *bad* type antibodies react with foreign antigens, a battle occurs at various sites in the body.

Symptoms and dis-ease conditions vary with the individual, depending upon where the antigen/antibody battle is occurring, that is, depending upon what might be the *shock* organ for that child or person.

When the shock organ is the skin, one might experience such symptoms and conditions as itching, rash, hives, eczema, etc. When the battle occurs in the lungs, one might experience coughing, wheezing, asthma, an increased sensitivity to respiratory infections, etc. When the shock organ is the stomach or intestines, the individual might complain of abdominal pain, colic, vomiting, or diarrhea. When the battle occurs in the area of the kidneys and bladder, burning on urination, increased frequency of urination, or bedwetting may result. When the shock organ is the brain, headaches might result or **any** function of the brain might be affected adversely, such as difficulty concentrating, poor memory, learning disabilities, dyslexia, hyperactivity, depression, emotional instability, anger, hallucinations, schizophrenia, to name a few.

The following list of foods are well-known culprits as causative or aggravating dietary factors in the allergic reaction. It is imperative that the following food items be eliminated **completely** from the diet for at least 6 weeks. Symptoms or diseases which may be expressions of, the result of, and/or aggravated by an allergic reaction may be expected to disappear almost immediately in some situations or may take as long as several weeks or months in others. The time factor would depend upon the condition, the organ involved, the time it would take to eliminate the allergen (or toxin) from the system, the ability of the body to repair the damage already done, and the degree to which the body (or organ) has become dependent (addicted) to the toxin or chemical. With some food ingredients, such as sugar, the body is not allergic to the sugar **per se**, but may instead become dependent or addicted to it. Sugar tends to increase the metabolic rate and would have a tendency to speed up any potential allergic reaction. In addition, sugar may itself be the direct causative factor in such conditions as hyperactivity or an aggravating factor in a situation such as dyslexia.

The No-No list of foods

— Sugar and sugar-containing foods (includes honey and dried fruits, such as raisins)
— Milk and milk products: cheese, ice cream, yogurt, etc.
— Caffeine-containing drinks and foods: coffee, tea, chocolate, and cola (some of the so-called "uncolas" have caffeine added to them)
— Citrus fruits and drinks: oranges, grapefruit, etc.
— Nuts and peanuts
— Eggs and beef
— Food additives: artificial flavors and colors, sweeteners, preservatives.

Feingold also implicates fruits and vegetables containing *salicylates* as causative dietary factors in hyperactivity. Natural *salicylate*-containing foods and substances include:

almonds	mint, oil of wintergreen
apples	peaches
apricots	pepper, green bell
aspirin	and chili
berries	plums and prunes
cherries	rose hips
cider and	spices: cloves, chili
cider vinegar	powder, cream
coffee	of tartar, ginger
cucumbers (pickles)	tangerines
currants	tangelos
grapes (raisins)	tea
nectarines	tomatoes
oranges	wine and wine vinegar

According to Feingold the following non-salicylate-containing fruits are permitted: avocado, bananas, coconut, dates, grapefruit, lemons, melons, papaya, pears, pineapple, and rhubarb. (How anyone can eat rhubarb without adding the greatest dietary causative factor in hyperactivity — sugar — is beyond me!)

We are not yet convinced that *endogenous* salicylate — that found naturally in foods — is the real culprit. From our observations we are now beginning to believe that hyperactivity is related to the amount of sugar consumed with some fruits such as grapes, raisins, berries, etc., to other substances such as caffeine in coffee and tea, and to allergy with some foods such as almonds, oranges, tomatoes, etc.

As mentioned earlier, we recommend **complete** elimination from the diet of the foods and substances noted in the **No-No List** for at least 6

EFFECTS OF DIET

weeks. Care must be exercised in feeding children fruits and fruit juices because of the increased amount of sugar consumed by eating them (as one of the *case histories* described below demonstrates).

After the child responds to this elimination diet, if the parents wish, they may reintroduce a single food at a time to determine the culprit food(s).

Be aware that many prescription and non-prescription drugs and medicines (e.g., antibiotics, cough preparations, etc.) contain both sugars and artificial colors and flavors. Such medicines should be used only when necessary to treat severe conditions.

Case histories

The following case histories and anecdotes serve to illustrate how allergy plays a part in childhood dis-ease and behavior problems.

J.R.: a case of bedwetting related to milk. The first time I saw J.R. was when he was 7 years old. One of his mother's complaints was that he was a bedwetter. In fact, he was lucky if he had one or two dry beds per month!

After completing the *conventional* medical workup and finding nothing which would pinpoint a cause, we attempted to tackle the problem through self-hypnosis. There was a group in one of the well-known Children's Hospital Centers advocating self-hypnosis as a technique to solve bedwetting: a report was published indicating that it was effective in about 70% of cases. Unfortunately, J.R. was in the 30% who did not respond.

I continued to see J.R. over the years for other sundry ailments, and he and his family learned to live with his bedwetting. When he was 14 years old, his father asked whether I thought that his son would be helped by attending a meditation course our Center sponsored. At age 14, J.R. was still wetting the bed at night, having only about one to two dry beds per month. In fact, this problem was interfering with his social life: he was unable to go away to Boy Scout camp; he would not stay overnight at friends' houses. I replied that I thought the course might help. What we teach is not much different from self-hypnosis, but since he was now 7 years older, he might now succeed where he had failed before. Besides, the course involves an holistic approach, and the child would be asked to try diet changes which would certainly help. I asked the father how much milk the child drank. His reply: "About 6 glasses daily." Since the course was not scheduled again for 4 weeks, I asked the father to stop feeding his son milk completely until he took the course.

I had not heard from the family for three and a half weeks. Two days before the course, I telephoned J.R.'s mother to ask whether they wished to have their son enroll. Her answer was "no." Two days after J.R. stopped drinking milk he **completely** ceased bedwetting. They thanked me and indicated their appreciation for having suggested stopping the milk.

B.D.: another case of bedwetting related to milk. One Tuesday a mother brought her 8-year-old son into the office for an unrelated illness. After examining the child and prescribing a course of treatment, she asked if I had time to talk with her. I replied, "Yes."

She told me that several weeks before she had seen on TV a man who suggested an association between bedwetting and drinking milk. This mother said: "You know, Dr. Tauraso, I stopped feeding my child milk, and he stopped wetting his bed immediately! He used to wet his bed every night!" There was a pause. She continued, "I sure wish I had listened to you a year and a half ago when you suggested that I try eliminating milk from the diet." I asked her why she had not followed my earlier advice. She made a gesture to indicate that maybe I had not been in full control of *my* senses when I made the suggestion. I decided to help her out. I said: "You thought I was crazy, didn't you? You thought I was some kooky physician, didn't you?" She replied: "To tell you the truth, I did! We have always been told that milk is the perfect food. Then you come along saying that milk may cause numerous problems. No one else in town talked about it. So I thought you weren't all together on the milk bit." I pointed my finger at her and said with a determined gleam in my eye: "And for your sins, you had to change all those wet sheets!" She laughed. I laughed.

I asked who the expert was she saw on TV. Her reply was that it was a well-known actor who did short TV spots on health-related matters. She mentioned his name. I replied that I bowed to this actor's intelligence in the matter but more so to his superior gift for convincing others. I said this, of course, with *tongue-in-cheek!*

What did I expect? Our community is a farming community **primarily** concerned with raising dairy cows. The whole community — as it is everywhere else in the United States — is bombarded with advertising about the most perfect food — milk. When someone comes along to shatter these myths, the average individual will not readily accept the new message.

M.M.: a case of hyperactivity related to an exquisite sensitivity to sugar. M.M. was 5 years old when his mother enrolled him in our T-H-E-M-E Positive Attitude Training Camp because of hyperactivity and difficulty in learning at school. M.M. did well and responded to a proper diet and relaxation/positive mental imagery exercises. He initially did well during the succeeding school year but at times seemed to regress to his previous usual hyperactive self.

The mother enrolled him in the camp the following summer. It appeared to us that M.M. was worse than he was when he first attended the camp the year previously. We searched for an explanation.

M.M. liked to eat fruit, sometimes eating 4 to 6 pieces per day. We suggested that he be taken off fruit entirely. The child's mother resisted. She insisted: "He likes fruit. His eating fruit cannot contribute to his behavior. I won't eliminate fruit from his diet." I replied: "So be it. I advise. You, the mother, decide."

Several weeks later she telephoned complaining that M.M. would not sit still in class nor during the relaxation session she has with him. I replied that I would not continue to advise her if she chose to select what she would ultimately try; in addition her unwillingness to cooperate interfered with the therapy I suggested and maybe she ought to seek out another physician she had more faith in. She replied that she would try for 30 days to eliminate fruit.

Several weeks later she telephoned again. She admitted that it was hard to believe, but that M.M. just was unable to tolerate any fruit on a daily basis. He appeared not to be affected by an occasional piece of fruit.

In my opinion, M.M. was not allergic per se to **all**

fruit, but that he was exquisitely sensitive to the quantity of sugar in most fruit. He is now doing well in school and at home. He appears happy. His parents are happy. The home is calm.

R.S.: a case of schizophrenia controlled by diet and vitamins. R.S. was a 23-year-old girl who at age 16 took LSD on 4 separate occasions. She had also experimented with *speed* and stelazine, marijuana, and 4 to 8 times with *angel dust*. She had been raped at age 16 by two men and again at age 21. Since age 16 and after having taken the above drugs, she had spent better than 90% of her life in mental institutions with a diagnosis of paranoid schizophrenia. Her mother wished to explore an holistic approach to possibly healing her daughter and asked whether we would help.

At that time, R.S. was taking several medications (Prolixin, Cogentin, and Navane) to control her hallucinations. Although her hallucinations were still almost constant, she apparently was less fearful of them while on the medications. Five months before she had a glucose tolerance test which suggested *hyperglycemia.*

We repeated the glucose tolerance test and demonstrated *hypoglycemia.* Hair analysis revealed a toxic amount of arsenic **and** an abnormally high but not toxic level of lead and cadmium in her system. All other mineral nutrients were low except for lithium which was abnormally high and selenium which was normal. She had been on lithium carbonate several months previously to control depression.

We attempted to map out a diet and vitamin program for R.S., but the State Hospital she was committed to would not cooperate. The authorities there felt that such an approach was both worthless and ridiculous to consider.

Her mother signed her out against hospital advice and R.S. was admitted to our Center for an experimental period of one month. We discontinued her medications, started her on an hypoallergenic natural foods diet, and initiated megavitamin therapy. Her hallucinations decreased in frequency with each successive day and stopped entirely 7 days later. On one occasion while out on an afternoon excursion, she drank a cup of coffee with sugar and cream. That evening R.S. ran around the Center laughing and yelling, obviously having one hallucination after another. The following morning she exhibited no such behavior and has not since.

The main challenge we are now facing with R.S. involves teaching her to mature psychologically. Her mental growth and development have not only been arrested, it has in fact regressed to a degree that she functions as a 13- or 14-year old. Her time spent in mental institutions has hardly been conducive to growth and maturity of her psyche. With the proper instruction we hope that R.S. will respond and become a useful participating member of society.

Schedule for meals

Introducing regularity in your children's lives helps establish **order**, essential to maintaining self-control. This is particularly true for developing a regular pattern of eating.

Since meal schedules are an individual matter which vary according to life styles, a general rule of thumb is suggested here. Let me mention a couple of different schools of thought concerning breakfast — one being that since the period of sleep uses this time for the rejuvenation of the body cells, morning (or whenever the period after sleep) is the time when the body has the highest usable energy in a 24-hour period. Therefore, a very **light** food intake, such as a serving of fresh fruit and/or fruit juice, would be in order so as not to draw from the energy level.

On the other hand, a **big** breakfast is said to fuel the body for a physically active day. An interesting point to consider is that the body's energy usually acts on priority, and when the food enters the body, the digestive process begins to operate automatically. There is a school of thought which advises us to *eat breakfast like a king, lunch like a prince, and dinner like a pauper.* The average individual is most active in the morning. Eating a large breakfast will result in more calorie energy at a time when it is most needed. Evening is usually a time of decreased physical activity, and less food should probably be consumed then. Excessive amounts of caloric energy produced within the body at a time when it is not really being used results in storage of that energy, usually as fat.

Obviously, with adults whose life style may be different, such as working a night shift, an evening performer, etc., the time of eating and amount of food consumed should be adjusted appropriately. Children's lives are usually not complicated in this way.

There are individual differences among children, however, which should be taken into consideration. Personally, throughout life I have felt more comfortable and alert not eating breakfast. One of my daughters is the same way. When she was a child one of her parents (identity to remain unknown to protect the guilty!) insisted that she eat a big breakfast which she would frequently vomit. Forcing **her** to eat a big breakfast was not the thing to do, no matter what cereal manufacturers would like us to do. When she grew older, she was able to convince her parents to respect that particular dietary habit. The challenge was resolved. The important point to establish in children is not when they eat what meal, but rather to follow the same pattern every day. The body gets tuned into a schedule and even expects to receive food at a particular time each day. An internal biologic clock gets set, and it is healthy to follow a set pattern.

Fasting

Although I do **not** recommend fasting for children, fasting is one of the best ways of developing self-discipline for adults. Developing self-responsibility for life's affairs depends upon developing self-discipline over both the body and mind. Fasting is being discussed here because some teenagers and young adults may wish to employ limited fasting at one time or another and it would be better if they knew more about it.

In many civilizations throughout history, reference is made to fasting as a way to lose weight and as a vehicle for man to strengthen his spirituality. Fasting lets the body know who is boss, because it establishes the mind and spirit as superior forces not to be easily influenced by bodily desires.

Although man derives much pleasure from his physical senses, overdoing it may actually deaden the experience. It is a well-established fact, for instance, that the more salt or sugar you use to season your food, the more you will require to experience an equivalent degree of the particular taste. This is why individuals develop the habit of adding more and more salt or sugar. This is what leads to addiction not only to certain food substances, but also to drugs and medications. If, on the other hand, you were to stop eating salt or sugar completely for several weeks, the taste buds would regenerate and become much more sensitive to small amounts of the appropriate flavoring substances.

In my opinion, the same situation exists with regard to overeating. This is a habit which develops from a lack of self-discipline about eating. In children the habit may result from custom within the home, the example set by older family members. We accept that eating is a pleasurable event. It was meant to be so. An overeater usually bolts his food down without chewing it well. He doesn't satisfy his hunger nor his eating senses enough so that he must eat more to achieve the pleasure he desires. As a result of overeating, he becomes obese, which further aggravates his self-image.

How does one fast? You don't need to go on a 40-day fast, although this has been done by One to achieve mastery over His carnal desires! Select a day of the week and instead of eating your usual meals, drink a glass of water or fruit juice for breakfast, eat a small cup of brown rice for lunch, and a cup of soup for dinner or supper. Double your exercise for that day. I will guarantee that not only on that day, but on the following day also, you will experience a fantastic emotional high. You will experience the feeling that you can do anything and everything. Try it. If you have any medical condition, consult your physician about how to handle fasting in your situation to insure that it is not contraindicated.

Young and older adults can begin to experience a change in their attitude toward themselves, family and friends, usually for the better because the body responds to natural health measures, as it does with anything else. Negative emotions of fear, anger and hatred are replaced by the positive emotions of love, tolerance, and joy. Negative emotions are the result of being out of control and lacking self-discipline. Much of the stress individuals experience comes from an unstable emotional state. Learning to be in control achieves mastery over one's emotions.

For children who wish to lose weight, one may consider employing a suitable dietary program in conjunction with PAT, including physical activity. Rather than resorting to employing strict fasts to achieve weight control, it would be far superior to put an overweight child on a good wholesome diet, eliminate the sugar, require that they chew each mouthful at least 50 times (for something as hard and chewy as brown rice and whole grain cereals, less for softer foods), and no second helpings, sugared desserts, and snacks (especially before bedtime).

Work with them using PAT to help them improve their self-confidence and develop better self-images. You and they will be rewarded by these efforts.

Conclusion

The food children eat influences their overall behavior. Certain toxic foods and chemical food additives interfere with the ability of many children to concentrate and pay attention. As a result their overall learning and memory faculties become short-circuited. Failing in school or being branded as hyperactive may cause them to express disciplinary problems which may further aggravate their poor learning and deteriorating self-image.

Attention to diet and employing PAT are prime considerations in solving these problems and returning to the natural state of individual being.

Nutrients for the garden

Plants require proper nourishment to grow, develop and come to fruition. The quality of the fruit greatly depends upon the quality of the food used to nourish the plant. One alternative is to supply chemical fertilizers. Another is to provide organic food such as that which Nature intends for the plant. The artificially-fertilized plant is basically weak, falling prey to many insects and infections and eventually requiring more chemicals to rid the garden of the pests. The naturally-grown plants are more robust and better able to withstand the insult of potential pests.

And so it is with the food we eat. Foods containing chemicals and foods altered so that the nutrients are destroyed weaken us. As a result, not only the body but also the mind and spirit are hindered in their growth. Natural foods feed the whole person and enable one to live more abundantly and healthfully.

CHAPTER 11

EFFECT OF EXERCISE ON MENTAL ATTITUDES

Introduction

Exercise affects our physical, mental, emotional, and spiritual health and our ability to develop and maintain health attitudes. This chapter describes how exercise affects metabolism and how metabolism affects mental attitudes.

General comments about metabolism

Metabolism is essentially the process by which food is converted into body-building protein, biochemicals (i.e., hormones, vitamins, enzymes, etc.) and energy.

Proper diet insures that we consume the vitamins and minerals the body is unable to manufacture. There are also essential amino-acids, the building blocks of protein which the body cannot make and, therefore, must be provided by the diet. The body is able to manufacture most of the amino-acids (except the "essential" ones), and hormones. However, it requires energy to do so. Although proteins can be converted into energy, most of the energy is derived from two major food sources: carbohydrates and fats.

Energy within living systems is measured in calories, which is defined as the amount of heat energy required to raise the temperature of one gram of water one degree centigrade. Carbohydrates and proteins contain 4 calories per gram and fats 8 calories per gram. One can readily appreciate that fats contain twice the calorie energy of carbohydrates and proteins.

Since carbohydrates and fats are the major sources of energy, a discussion of how they are metabolized is appropriate. Carbohydrates, which should make up the major portion of our food energy can be metabolized in one of two ways, either aerobically (a system requiring oxygen) or anaerobically (not requiring oxygen). Fats can **only** be metabolized aerobically.

Keep in mind that the body is a great conservationist. It will and does conserve the excess energy it produces by converting it either into glycogen, a complex animal carbohydrate, which can readily be reconverted to simple sugars for quick metabolism, or into fat, which usually gets stored in conspicuous places around the body and which is **not** readily reconverted into energy.

Aerobic vs. anaerobic exercise

Aerobic exercise is preferred to anaerobic because the former results in a metabolism which can easily process carbohydrates and fats. This is especially beneficial if you have a tendency toward being overweight and fat.

Children who are fat eventually become concerned about it. Friends and peers ridicule them. Their self-image is shattered and they become unhappy. Although the answer to the obesity problem may be simple, developing the self-discipline to carry out the solution may be more difficult.

The solution exists in following the dietary advice given in the previous chapter and combining this with a program of aerobic exercise. Describing in detail such a program is beyond the scope of this book. The reader is referred to our earlier book, *How To Benefit From Stress,* or other books on aerobic exercise.

Effect of exercise on physical, mental, emotional, and spiritual health

Physical exercise teaches the body the correct way to go. The efficiency of the cardiovascular system improves: the heart increases in size, resting heart rate decreases, and there is an increase in the *stroke* volume (i.e., the volume of blood pumped by a single contraction of the heart — the greater the *stroke* volume, the more efficient the heart). As a result, blood pressure usually decreases and stabilizes. All the tissues and organs of the body receive more oxygen and the individual experiences physical vigor and strength, clarity of thinking, and a better overall health.

Lack of exercise results in anaerobic metabolism and an increase of lactic acid in the muscles. The lactic acid accumulation is the cause of muscle fatigue. When metabolism is mostly aerobic, lactic acid is not produced and the muscles do not experience true fatigue. This is the reason why long distance marathon runners seem to go on and on!

Anyone who regularly exercises admits to experiencing increased clarity of thinking following exercise. This most likely can be explained by increased oxygen supply to the brain, decreased lactic acid accumulation in the muscles, and *endorphin* production. (The emotional *joggers' high* of runners has been shown to be due to the production of *endorphins*.) The brain is very sensitive to oxygen. A lack of oxygen to the brain for 3 to 5 minutes usually results in irreversible brain damage. It would be reasonable to assume that anything which would increase blood flow to and oxygenation of the brain would result in better brain cell functioning. This appears to be the case.

Since our spirit reflects through our body, brain and mind, anything which would improve their function would also result in our spirit being uplifted.

School exercise programs

Although most schools have developed elaborate physical education (PE) departments, the quality of their programs leaves much to be desired. The emphasis on competitive sports and the *ego tripping* of many PE instructors result in children rejecting exercise as a way of life after graduation, not developing a long-term exercise program which would be beneficial for their general overall health. It should not be a graded subject.

School exercise programs should put an emphasis on teaching aerobics in the form of non-competitive sport. Exercise should and can be fun for children and instructors.

Conclusion

Physical activity does convince the body of the correct way to go and provides one of the goals leading to better health. A reasonable amount of regular physical activity increases the flow of blood to the tissues and actually rejuvenates the cells. It helps flush out the waste products of metabolism from the tissues. It relaxes the body.

Exercise not only relaxes the mind, it increases mental acuity as well. You begin to think more clearly. Along with this, emotions improve and the spirit within becomes more alive.

Parents should perform exercise together with their children. When families exercise together, they live favorably together!

THE GARDEN OF LIFE

Plants exercise too

A plant growing in a greenhouse, protected from the rigors of wind and rain, develops thin leaves and stems, and is not able to grow outside in the severe environment. Trees and plants which grow up exposed to the wind and rain develop stronger trunks, stems and leaves. Natural outdoor exercise enables the plants to grow stronger and more hardy.

Children respond similarly to exercise. Increased activity causes the muscles to develop and the bones to become more sturdy. A healthy body encourages a healthy mind and nurtures a vital spirit.

CHAPTER 12

SPIRITUAL TRAINING

Introduction

A common assumption about spiritual training is that if a child goes to Church School for an hour each week or takes some catechetical classes, he or she is receiving sufficient and proper training. The fallacy of this assumption is easily seen when we realize the number of hours and years a child spends in secular education.

Another misconception is that when a child is received into the church through confirmation, usually before 14 years of age, he or she "graduates" and needs no more formal spiritual training. Actually, we never graduate or finish spiritual training for such learning goes on throughout our entire life.

Basic factors in spiritual training

Certainly one of the most important factors in the spiritual training and growth of a child is the attitude and behavior of parents concerning spiritual realities. When parents live out their faith, children are much more likely to follow their example. The converse is also true. This means that the parents not only participate in formal religious education and worship, but also that they be a loving and listening presence. More than one child has run away from home because parents have not expressed love or really listened to what their children were saying. There is a divine current that flows through the minds and hearts of children that adults need to hear. That current brings a different rhythm to life — a rhythm that often leads to stillness, silence and deep reflection where one discovers the heart of God.

Regularity, or discipline, is very important in spiritual growth. The adage that practice makes perfect is as true in the life of the spirit as in any other area of living. Regular prayers with children, Bible reading and grace at meals are good habits that nurture the soul.

The place of prayer in spiritual training is paramount. Prayer is the conscious unfoldment of self for the reception of the vivifying, healing and developing influence of spirit. Prayer illumines, clarifies, and reinforces faith, grants knowledge of our motives and helps to unify these motives, activates latent power and energy within, releases repressions. Prayer helps us to be aware of needs and realities, promotes trust, leads to dedication and facilitates decision-making. Prayer sensitizes us to the hurts and needs of others and lifts us out of our guarded ghettos to cosmic consciousness. Prayer aids in self-realization — *we know who we are when we know Whose we are* — and in self-integration.

Most persons do not recognize these values of prayer, know little about the many dimensions and techniques of prayer, and practice prayer only sporadically.

SPIRITUAL TRAINING

The following statements are some practical "starters" for the life of prayer. After reading these, write some of your own statements and reflect on them.
— Corporate prayer is powerful.
— Detachment, relaxation, deep breathing can facilitate prayer.
— Using acting words in your prayers such as flow, envelop, bathe, penetrate with light, breathe, create good and helpful images and energies.
— Pray with a pencil. Write down your prayers and keep visible until carried into action.
— Offer "flash" prayers for those in emergency situations.
— Pray with the body — as you walk or exercise.
— Saturate the mind with the Scripture.
— Think of God at least one second each minute.
— Image Christ or some other great soul in or near those for whom you pray.

Children and adults often ask about "unanswered" prayers. Although we cannot always explain why some prayers seem to be unanswered, sometimes the following reasons are satisfying to the questioner.
— We don't know all of God's laws and workings.
— Rational and scientific explanations do not encompass all of reality.
— Our prayers may be bound by our own dark motives.
— Our lives are lived in community. A specific prayer, if answered, may be harmful to many others.
— Our prayers can be limited by our own wrongdoing.
— Some prayers God must not answer, specifically

those that go against natural and spiritual laws. There are vast realms where God must not substitute our wish for His plan.
— We may not be ready to receive the gift we desire in our prayer.
— Although the specific petition may not be answered, the person can be answered.

Nature teaches us so much about life. The parts and functions of our bodies, the stars, seas, trees, flowers, animals, and insects all can be as mirrors reflecting aspects of the Creator and contribute to our spiritual maturity. Much spiritual teaching by the masters comes from nature. The parables of Jesus are good examples. Children can be taught spiritual truths and gain appreciation for God's creation from experiences in nature.

These opportunities to teach about spiritual realities from nature are always present. The caterpillar changing to a butterfly can be used to share thoughts with a child about death and life after death. Light from the sun, which causes plants to grow, can exemplify God's warm love that enables us to grow more loving. The mother cat carrying her kittens by the scruff of the neck can symbolize God's carrying us, in our helplessness, by His grace and power. Dirty, melting snow being drawn up, by evaporation, into clouds by the sun and sent down again pure and white, can signify the cleansing power in our lives of God's forgiving love. Water, as a still lake, bubbling brook, or surging sea, can offer many metaphors about the spiritual life. The possibilities for teaching spiritual truths through examples from nature are manifold.

A significant subject for teaching spiritual truths from natural processes is that of human sexuality.

The growing body is an excellent classroom or laboratory for learning about the life of the spirit. Birth, puberty, adolescence, young and old adulthood are more than biological and psychological dynamics in our lives. We are all involved in sexuality from the womb to the tomb. Human sexuality includes the bodily functions, emotions, mind, values, and social relations, all of which have implications for the spiritual life.

It might seem strange to link spiritual training with learnings and experiences in human sexuality. But when we take seriously the importance of sexuality and spirituality, and consider their interrelationship, we can appreciate this approach to spiritual training. Both sexuality and spirituality involve creativity, are powerful universal energies, move persons toward communion and union, and provide roots and fruits of love.

The Bible is an invaluable resource for spiritual training. Today there are many good, experiential approaches to Bible study that can be adapted to children of all ages. Major Christian denominations have excellent materials for spiritual nurture and samples are easily obtained from denominational publishing houses. The same is true of good devotional reading material.

One method of studying Scripture is combining Scripture reading with meditation. Select a passage in Scripture and then imagine yourself in and of the situation about which you are reading. You visualize the scene, being (with) the person or persons, and feel the action. This is the emotional involvement in the reading. The second step involves the intellect as you consider the meaning of the passage in general and the particular meaning for yourself. The third step is the act of the will in which you ponder the question of what this passage is demanding of you right now. The final step is your resolve to take some specific action. This kind of Bible study is holistic and realistic and can be done alone or with others.

Summer camps and retreats of various kinds help to nurture the child's spirit. Usually these programs combine the spiritual training with other aspects of holistic life — exercise, diet, mental activity — and thereby bring a wholesome and balanced living experience to the child. Many children have received a spiritual awakening through these camp and retreat experiences.

Another area of spiritual training is that of dream analyses and intrepretation. Throughout history lives have been enriched, even saved, through dreams. Numerous examples are in the Bible. Today serious research is being done in scientific and religious circles concerning the importance of dreams in the growth of the whole person. Spiritual insights and inspiration are frequently obtained through sharing our dreams with others, especially those close to us. Family sharing of dreams each morning is practiced by some cultures to great advantage, and the same can happen to persons in any culture if the commitment is made to work with dreams.

Techniques for dream interpretation vary but most usually contain some or all of the following processes:

1. Clarifying the feelings in the dream. This is more than just finding out how the dreamer feels about the dream. Rather, it is an attempt to expose the full spectrum of feelings in the dream.
2. Extracting the theme of the dream, which is a

summary of the main plot of the dream or a basic statement of its action.
3. Ascertaining the meaning of the dream symbols, including symbol amplification, which is an attempt to expand the dreamer's associations to, and familiarity with, the symbol.
4. Arriving at a preliminary understanding which provides a framework for the dream to take on a meaning.
5. Applying the dream to daily life.

Consideration of death and life after death can be an important factor in spiritual training. Many adults and parents need to come to terms with this aspect of their own lives before they can help children. The following suggestions are offered as ways of developing positive attitudes and feelings about facing death and beyond:
1. Examine your fears and superstitions about death in general and your own death in particular.
2. Reflect on the meaning of and your relationship to time. What is eternity? Is any death untimely? How long does it take to fulfill a life's purpose? What would you do if you knew for certain you had one month to live?
3. Study some good writings about death and life after death, especially Scripture.
4. Make special efforts to develop sensitive acquaintances with those who are dying, such as the terminally ill and the chronically ill, the elderly. Move toward rather than away from the dying.
5. Attend funerals and be with the bereaved. Your presence, even in silence, is power for you and the grieving.
6. Make your will and be open to helping others do this.

7. Participate in some death-centered programs, e.g., self-awareness groups, hospices, Make Today Count, Widow to Widow, etc.
8. Reflect on death in your spiritual journey and faith, especially noting the significance of resurrection in your thoughts, words and deeds.

As you acquire confidence and strength in your own facing of death, so will you better be able to communicate these positive attitudes to children.

Intergenerational relationships can be a form of spiritual enlightenment. The gifts of the elderly are often spiritual ones that are gained through many years of living. Also, children sometimes find in older persons a hero who inspires, encourages and enables them to discover their genius within. Grandparents and other older relatives and friends are important for a child's total development.

Literature such as nursery rhymes, fairy tales, myths, legends, and stories are powerful vehicles for spiritual learnings. Reverence, respect, justice, truth, fairness, and kindness are frequently portrayed in picturesque fashion that gains the attention of children. When sharing these stories and experiences with children, we shall accomplish much toward their spiritual understanding if the moral and ethical lessons are stressed.

Just as the child's mind is fertile and flexible, so is the child's spirit. Fantasies, imaginations, visualizations and creative play are part of the child's nature and these should be encouraged when they are positive and fruitful. Too often a child's spirit is quenched by such expressions as, "It's just your imagination," "Don't bother me with that silliness," or "The devil will get you if you don't stop such talk." Adults have much to learn from children, and one of the most important learnings is to be open to all possibilities and not to cut off "ridiculous" or "far out" articulations and actions of children.

Finally, one of the greatest spiritual gifts we can give to children is hope. Hope is the affirmation that the overwhelming brutality of facts that oppress and repress is not the last word — that the future frontiers of the possible are not determined by the limits of the present actual, and that in miraculous and unexpected ways life is preparing the creative events which open the way to freedom and to the actualizing of the genius that lies within each child.

Let us then plant oak trees even though we may never gather acorns. Let us live inspired by the love of what or whom we shall never see. This is the secret key to eternity, the leap of faith, the risking and challenging of loving deeply and responsibly. It is the refusal to let the creative act, the genius, be dissolved away in the now sense experience. It is the firm commitment to the future of the children of the world, children who teach us what commitment means. Such love, hope, faith and commitment are what give prophets, revolutionaries, saints, and geniuses the courage to both live and die for the future they envisage.

A garden reflects the spirit of the master gardener

A wise man once said that a garden reflects the thoughts and consciousness of the gardener. This is true. Two individuals growing plants in adjacent plots of land may reap crops of totally different qualities. The better quality crops are said to be grown by the individual with the **green thumb.** *All of us have a* **green thumb** *but all do not demonstrate it because of the lack of awareness and training.*

All in the garden of life are endowed with spirits, and the fruits of life depend upon how aware and how appreciative one is of the Spirit life-force. Those who engage in spiritual disciplines will experience rich, abundant and lasting harvests.

CHAPTER 13

RESPONSIBILITY OF PARENTS

Introduction

Although parents seem to have a more varied job description than any other profession, it is probably the only profession which requires and acquires its subject credits through an osmotic process from generations of family laboratory experimentation! Archives of data have been collected, tried, eliminated, recycled, etc., and to date, no two humans have identical computers to view through. Consequently, there are no hard and fast rules, routine programs, steps, and formulas to guarantee a *royal straight flush* in child rearing, even when dealing from a stacked deck.

However, as the culture is placed under the microscope after incubation to see what is cooking, so do parents see "what is cooking" as a result of their efforts. So let us see what is crawling around through this high-powered scope and share our feelings!

Parents are considered the prime figures of authority and responsibility in raising children. Other individuals such as teachers, school principals, other instructors (i.e., dance, music), coaches, policemen, the state, etc., serve as temporary supervisors of children's welfare, but they **all** derive their authority from the parents.

In my experience as a pediatrician counselling parents on their children's learning disabilities and behavior problems, I frequently encounter the parents blaming the school for some inadequacy in their children's development, or the state for not providing a particular service, or some other group of individuals or institutions. Teachers and principals frequently blame the parent. And so, there is a psychological tug-of-war with the child suffering in between or gloating over his victory. Most frequently, one parent is pointing the accusatory finger at the other parent.

The purpose of the next two chapters is to describe the delineation of authority and responsibilities and suggest ways by which everyone involved might work harmoniously toward the goal of teaching and guiding children to learn how to develop their innate God-given talents and abilities for positive growth and development.

General aspects

To continue in this theme it is important to establish order in the delineation of authority and responsibilities. First, children who learn attitudes and behavior primarily by example will develop order in their lives if they see order in the lives of those in the authority structure around them. They can learn to respond to order with order, and this becomes an early lesson in learning self-discipline.

Second, confusion can be prevented if all authority figures work together and act in unison without accusatory behavior in teaching children.

This will also prevent being duped by the manipulative games of children. It is normal behavior for children to be manipulative as they learn to test the boundaries of **their** own authority over themselves. The challenge arises with existing supervisory authority (i.e., parents, teachers, etc.) who must recognize this behavior of children, analyze it, and determine when a child might be ready to assume a particular level of authority and responsibility over himself.

Parents and all those temporary authority figures must learn to work as a team. Parents who see themselves tired from the drudgery of raising their children are frequently all too willing to leave it to the teachers or the schools. Parents are responsible for their children's overall education, not teachers. Teachers are responsible in the conduct of this charge. Parents **must** get involved with teaching their children those subjects that have moral and spiritual overtones (e.g., sex education) or develop a team effort with their minister and church. This should not be left up to teachers whose moral values you, the parent, don't know about. If you are an involved parent and have investigated the qualifications and moral attitudes of the teacher and conclude that everything is according to what you consider correct, then by all means **delegate** the authority to perform this task to the teacher.

Authority **must** be firm and kind and not oppressive and cruel.

Preparation for life outside the home

A major responsibility of parents is to prepare their children for life **outside** the home. An all too common error of parents is overprotecting their children. An overprotected child grows up fearful and afraid of new encounters, adventure, and living. The child's mind is a very logical one. Why are my parents protecting me? There must be something out there my parents are protecting me from. What is it? **Overprotection is one of the greatest stumbling blocks in teaching children positive attitudes.** The reason is that overprotection generates fear within a child's mind and *fear and positive attitudes are incompatible.*

Fear is the most powerful of the negative emotions and does more to destroy an individual from within (ref. *How to Benefit from Stress,* see Glossary.) This process is one of self-destruction.

Teach children to be fearless, to welcome the ever-changing adventure of life. Teach them how to climb a tree. So what it they break a leg! It will heal. It could be far worse to grow up fearing the tree. Teach them to move forward accepting the experiences of life as new adventures to enjoy. It could be far worse to grow up fearing life itself.

Use PAT techniques of affirmation so that both you and your children become fearless and strong. Employ positive mental imagery in meditation and see yourselves as masters of yourselves and mastering all about you. Convince your subconscious that you are strong. Believe it so that you experience it.

Mentioned earlier in the book were two of the biggest obstacles we create in our lives: ignorance and resistance to change. Teach your children not to be ignorant about themselves or their fellow human beings.

Prejudice is a form of ignorance. Develop and practice understanding and tolerance of everyone around you. Your children will learn from what they observe, from the example that you give them. Enlighten your children so that they grow up enlightened, not ignorant.

Resistance to change comes from a desire to be secure and stable. The Universe, God, everything around us are constantly changing forces. **The act of creation is still going on.** Asking to be secure and demanding stability is going counter to the forces of nature. You become out of touch with the rhythm of life. You are left behind as the world moves forward. If children are taught to fear change, they resist it throughout their lives. They fear uncertainty.

Teach your children to move forward against uncertainty with strength and vigor. Teach them to welcome change as their birthright, as a part of creation.

Teaching goal setting

Many individuals wander through life aimlessly going from nowhere to nowhere or moving along in a serpentine fashion not quite reaching anywhere. *Many go nowhere in life because they do not know where they are going.* They have no goals.

Goals must first be set before they can be reached. It is a form of order to set priorities. Learn to set down goals for what you want your children to learn. Then begin using the process.

With adults we recommend writing your goals down on paper. This helps crystallize them as they are moving from the mental to the physical reality. Write down the goals you hope to achieve in your lifetime. They can be general or specific or both. Preferably, general lifetime goals are preferred, goals that are constantly evolving and not those that are limited. For instance, if you set your mind to achieve a limited goal in your lifetime, perhaps becoming president of the company, it may well be that once you achieve this lifetime goal, you will then die! Do I make my point? The mind is most powerful and the Universe supportive to **all** your wishes. Insure that your programming does not accidentally include a mental self-destruct conclusion.

Write down those goals you wish to accomplish over the next year, by the next month, within the week, tomorrow, and today. Direct your mental energies to your goals. Pray that you will reach these goals **only** if no hurt nor harm besets anyone, *for the good of all concerned, no hurt, no harm to anyone,* as the Huna philosophy teaches. Believe in yourself and have faith that all will be accomplished according to God's will. Then, go out and work to make things happen. **Faith without works is dead** is as true now as it has been from time immemorial (ref. **Scientific Prayer** in *How to Benefit from Stress,* pp. 172-173, see Glossary.)

Learn to be flexible. There is no reason why after a day, week, or month you cannot change your goals. Life is an ever-evolving situation and, if you are in tune with the rhythm of life, you will be changing and growing into newer and higher levels of understanding. Goals may need to be modified to adjust to your new being.

One important feature of goal setting is to preserve silence. You need not share your goals with anyone. In fact, it is better that you don't. The negative thinking of others may interefere with your belief and cause your energy to be dissipated. You may share your dream **after** it becomes a conscious reality. If on the other hand you and others share the same goal, possibly a joint effort, then by all means meditate together, pool your concerted energies, and crystallize your imagery into physical reality.

Now that you have accomplished this for yourself, share the principles with your children. Teach them to set goals, to write them out when they are old enough. Their lifetime goals can be very general. With very young children, teach them goal setting by example. They will learn as they listen to you talk and as they observe how you act and what you do. With older children and young adults, inquire as to what they desire to be and do with their lives. This is responsible business. Remember it is **their** goals you wish to explore, not yours. But, on the other hand, you are there as a guide and counsellor with the responsibility to teach them to be responsible.

Authority support

Another responsibility of parents is to be supportive of delegated authority. Support teachers and principals in carrying out their duties to educate your children.

If your child comes home with a "tale of woe" about a teacher or the principal, do you rise up in blind self-righteous indignation ready to trample the teacher because *your child is always right?* Or do you listen to your child, then listen to the teacher, and **together** with the teacher decide as objectively as you both can to handle the situation in the best interests of the child? Obviously, the latter is preferred. Of course, there will be times when parent and teacher will not agree. Then the ultimate responsiblity is on the parent.

Teach children to view authority as kind and to support others who dedicate their talents and lives to help others. Teach children to play constructive life games and not those which tend to be disruptive to oneself. Teach them to be responsive to reasonable authority so that situations over which they will have increasing authority will respond to them in like manner. A parent who is responsive to God's authority can expect that his children will be responsive to his. Children who are responsive to the authority of God and their parents can expect that their subordinates and children in due time will be responsive to them.

PAT should include establishing some form of order in children's lives so that they will be in tune with the order in the universe.

Application of a PAT program

Parents are responsible for supplying all that is necessary for their children's optimal physical growth and development. They are also responsible for their children's mental and spiritual growth and development.

The human mind is one of the most important and unique creations. Through the mind an individual's spirit is allowed to manifest here on the physical plane. The mind and brain function as a biocomputer with properties much like those computers made by man. **What comes out of our minds is directly related to what goes in.** Herein lies the crux behind the reason why children should be taught positive attitudes; that is, so that they can grow up to be positive, act positively, and experience the positive side of life. It is learning how to polarize oneself toward constructive rather than destructive creation.

Parents can extract from this book or from other sources useful ideas which they can apply in teaching their children how to view life, so that they can get the most out of it. Waiting until one gets older is not the best time to achieve positive attitudes, although it can be done at any time. Doing it early helps establish good habits which are as hard to break as bad habits. So devise a program to help your children learn good habits which they can use and benefit from throughout life.

The garden teachers

Although nature provides all of the necessary ingredients (soil, nutrients, seed, water, sunlight), the gardener must utilize these ingredients wisely for optimal plant growth and development. The young farmer or gardener is usually inexperienced and benefits greatly from the instruction of those more experienced.

Parents have a special responsibility to utilize all of the ingredients given to them to promote optimal growth for their children. Each child is a precious and sacred gift — a tender plant that is entrusted to the parents for awhile. No effort is too great to insure that the child is given the opportunity and privilege to enjoy a healthy and happy life.

CHAPTER 14

RESPONSIBILITY OF TEACHERS AND SCHOOL SYSTEM

Introduction

Teachers are the second most important influence in the lives of children. As mentioned earlier in Chapter 7, children spend a considerable amount of time (50 to 60 percent of their waking hours during the week) in school or involved with school-related events and activities, exposed to the influences of teachers, coaches, principals (in this chapter the term *teachers* will apply to all three unless otherwise indicated).

Schools are charged with the responsibilitiy of educating children and training them to think and use their minds for self-development. How well do they perform this task and do they succeed?

This chapter attempts to answer these questions by analyzing and evaluating some aspects of the teaching environment and the study habits of children. The responsibilities of teachers to prevent, detect, and handle children with so-called learning disabilities (e.g., dyslexia, poor memory, poor self-image, etc.) are also discussed.

General aspects

The challenges faced by teachers in our modern-day schools are enormous. On the one hand, they deal with students, many of whom would try even Job's patience, especially some of the older ones. On the other hand, teachers are expected to deal with the ever-increasing bureaucracy of the school administration and with parents, many of whom haven't yet graduated from mental kindergarten! And, hopefully, with the wisdom of Alexander the Great as he cut the Gordian knot, teachers must **teach and do it right the first time**.

Discipline and the support of discipline leaves much to be desired as the average teacher considers it an insurmountable issue, at best, and shies away from being a disciplinarian. Discipline is required any time you are at the helm of a ship attempting to sail a straight course. Teaching would be a delightful experience if everyone who comes into the classroom were intent on learning. It befalls the teacher to stimulate and inspire students to work. This goal **is** reached often, but there are always a few students who require more force and persuasion to get them to work. The teacher is faced with this challenge.

In school, children become aware, probably for the first time for many, that they have a brain and a mind. They learn about memory and are told what to put into it. Later they are asked to recall it at test time. Most of the time they are not told why they must learn a subject, but only that they must because it is required. Many teachers themselves don't know why they are teaching a subject. They may be doing so only because they chose or were ordered to. And so confusion breeds confusion.

Modern children are the most **factually** enlightened in history. As students, we are taught subject not only for their content, but for exercising our mental faculties. Teaching children why they are learning a subject would help in developing their motivation. Motivation is a very important element in the learning process, especially if learning is to be an holistic experience. **Motivation** is an aspect of a person's will and drive which helps him focus and direct energy mentally at first, followed by physical and eventually spiritual energies.

One of the teacher's responsibilities is to instill purpose in school children, to motivate them to learn to develop their minds. Memorizing a particular poem (e.g., Francis Thompson's *The Hound of Heaven*) is really unimportant. The important thing is learning how to develop and use the faculty of memory. Teaching overall concepts of learning in addition to details of a particular subject identifies the true teacher from a technician who tends to emphasize only the latter. The student will eventually realize what is really important and decide for himself what he wishes to recall. The facts will work their way in as part of the game of learning.

Learning should be a game for children. They like to play games. The mind likes games. There are teachers who are able to take what are generally considered the driest subjects and present them in an exciting manner. Parents observe that most children complain about their teacher's inability to teach rather than about the subject matter. Creative teaching arouses the interests of students and stimulates the learning faculty.

Learning disabilities

One of the most frustrating challenges for teachers is how to handle children with so-called *learning disabilities*. At the outset, I would like to consider all of these children as having functional problems. Truly brain-damaged children usually don't get to a regular classroom. I will have more to say about these children because much can and has been done to open up more areas of their minds resulting in improved mental function. Considering learning disabilities as *functional* and *temporary* would tend to establish a positive attitude in teachers (and parents). This positive attitude will be psychically conveyed to the children, who, in turn, will overcome their learning challenges much more easily than if everyone is psychically programming a relatively hopeless situation.

Children pick up the psychic thoughts of those around them through their as yet unadulterated sensing mechanisms. Whether you would like to believe it or not, please do! Experiments in the laboratory are confirming the fact that thought energy not only exists but it can and is conveyed psychically to those around us. The closer you are to other individuals, the more you will exchange energy with them. It is possible to influence their thoughts and they yours.

This may be the reason why some teachers are more effective than others in helping these children, or any other children for that matter. These teachers tune into the spiritual perfection within children. They convey this thought and **picture** to the child, and the child begins to act accordingly.

In our T-H-E-M-E Positive Attitude Training Camps the staff is oriented to be positive and creative. With this attitude, and much patience, and understanding, many lives take on new meaning. This is especially true when teachers and parents are in alignment.

Considering all those children who experience difficulties with the learning experience, from those exhibiting poor concentration and memory to dyslexic and hyperactive children, the numbers are staggering. I will try to describe and analyze some of these situations, starting with the mildest leading up to the more severe conditions. We will try to build a ladder of challenges and contributing circumstances. Almost everything which is discussed concerning children with the mildest difficulties will apply to those with more severe challenges. Suggestions for prevention and treatment will follow in the next section.

Poor concentration probably leads the list of challenges facing almost everyone from time to time. Many adults attend our T-H-E-M-E Training Seminars because they have difficulty concentrating. It is a by-product of the unconscious training which begins early in life, and it continues to exist for years unless, or course, it is detected and handled somehow.

Difficulty in concentrating is more than just annoying. It can prevent one from achieving goals: passing a test, graduating with high grades, achieving in sports, getting a job or promotion, being successful financially, achieving happiness. Unachieved goals can frustrate anyone, and repeated failures may seriously erode self-esteem and feelings of self-worth.

This difficulty in concentrating begins in childhood as a bad habit and should be corrected as soon as it is noticed. Better yet, as with all mental related challenges, would be to prevent it.

Children who experience difficulty in concentration may be seen staring in space, diverting their attention everywhere but nowhere, fidgeting in their chairs, and getting into mischief. As a result of this behavior, these children do poorly in their studies, and get poor grades or fail. At this point they may view themselves as failures, which may lead to loss of self-esteem, further aggravating their ability to concentrate and learn.

Poor memory is another frustrating situation plaguing individuals of all ages and having its origins in childhood. According to Bruno First, the famed memory expert who devised those now famous *Memory Pegs,* there are two prerequisites to good memory: a relaxed mind and learning ways to put facts into memory by association. When the mind is relaxed, information flows readily from it. Many who are uptight during exams experience temporary loss of memory during the test, and after it is over and they are relaxed again, they can again remember what they had forgotten earlier.

As with all mental faculties, memory improves with use. It is even more enhanced with motivation.

Another aspect is the fact that if you believe you have a poor memory and continue to affirm, "I have a poor memory," "My memory is bad," "My memory is failing," or "I can't remember," your mind will believe it. Any attempts to improve memory will occur only after changing the input, i.e., your self-image. Affirmations work to the degree they are repeated or reinforced. Many individuals perpetuate negative conditions by affirmation. Wtih the same effort why not continuously reinforce positive situations?

Encourage children to reaffirm their self-capabilities and watch their self-image and performance improve.

Dyslexia (reading disability) is a much more serious condition that can have many causes. One suggested cause is a malfunctioning or "immature" *corpus callosum* (a mass of nerve fibers connecting the two sides of the brain). Dyslexia can also be caused by an inability to process speech sounds, either the result of dysfunction in the LB or a failure to process spatial information such as printed words, probably an RB dysfunction. Both these causes suggest a failure to integrate information between left and right brain. Another cause may be difficulty in synthesizing information from two or more regions on one side of the brain, such as visual, spatial, and auditory (hearing) stimuli. Many dyslexic children exhibit visual difficulties, such as farsightedness and inability to maintain binocular fixation, to name a few.

Children with reading disabilities (dyslexia) are poor readers by definition. They may have difficulty in perceiving letters or words in their proper order; they may exhibit mirror vision (very rare).

These children do not have any identifiable brain lesions other than the dysfunctional situations described above. *Childhood dyslexia is not a dis-ease in the usual sense.* Such children are actually slow in maturing and will eventually outgrow their reading problem.

The important point for teachers and the school system is to detect the dyslexic child early through his reading ability.

Hyperactivity *(hyperkinesis)* is a condition characterized by excessive movement (fidgeting, nervousness), poor attention span and lack of concentration. Many hyperkinetic children become disciplinary problems since they easily do not listen very well, which is probably related to their inability to pay attention to commands. When manifested in the toddler stage, hyperactive children are always on the go, frequently wander away from home, get into trouble around the house, and don't listen to their parents. Later in school this excessive nervous activity translates into difficulty in learning, poor memory, poor achievement and disruptiveness.

Hyperactive children usually have above average I.Q.s, which confuses interpretation because of their poor school performance.

Unlike the children exhibiting the other learning difficulties described above, hyperkinetic children usually are taking prescribed drugs, (e.g., dexedrine, ritalin) which calm them down. As a result, their attention span is increased and they perform average work in school. Although drugs used to be the answer, this condition can virtually be cured by diet and PAT.

Prevention and treatment of learning disabilities

Our approach to the handling of children with learning disabilities is based on a sound health philosophy which proposes that the mind functions in a unique way similar to a computer, that is depends upon the physical brain for input of information through the physical senses and for expression, and that it can create throughts and ideas through the employment of mental and spirit senses. The brain is dependent upon the rest of the body for life and is subject to all the influences of the physical world, such as diet, toxins, etc. Because of this, the functioning of the mind also is affected by situations affecting the physical body. What motivates the mind to express more than any other single factor is **belief**. Anything affecting this belief will affect mental reality initially and then in time physical reality (or expression).

A seemingly vague philosophy of generalizations such as this would probably have little meaning if it were not for the fact that this philosophy is the basis of the development of a system of Positive Attitude Training which involves the use of **affirmations** to create positive creative imaginings to develop belief, **meditation** to tap the high-energy mind power of the subconscious mind, and **positive mental imagery** to impress what it desired into the inner subconscious belief system and to crystallize thought into reality.

This in itself would be meaningless if it did not work. But, **it does work!**

First, all children including those with learning disabilities would benefit from a **good natural diet devoid of chemical additives** and avoidance of certain foods which naturally contain or are themselves psychotropic chemicals (e.g., sugar, caffeine).

Second, using PAT techniques described in Chapter 5, children can learn how to concentrate and improve memory, chiefly through special exercises. A primary function of PAT techniques is to develop confidence and belief in the child's own capabilities — a **must** in overcoming learning problems.

Third, the electrochemical energy tapped by using meditation will result in correcting the problems of RB/LB integration and other dysfunctions seen in the dyslexic child. In other words, brain function which usually requires X amount of energy in most children may require 10 X energy in the dyslexic child. It is recommended that dyslexic children undergo a complete medical evaluation to detect and correct any other physical defects such as poor or altered vision.

Fourth, hyperactive children can learn through PAT techniques to relax and see themselves as creative children.

Teachers can be oriented to implement these techniques, not only in the child who exhibits learning difficulties, but in all children in their classes so they will achieve optimum potential. Another benefit would be that children would be more relaxed generally, and consequently more manageable.

This approach to handling children with learning disabilities would be considered a form of treatment for those children already exhibiting symptoms and as preventive measures to others.

Development of self-esteem

This is mentioned in this chapter because many children who have difficulties in school soon develop challenges in their self-image. Doing poorly or failing subjects may cause them to view themselves as failures. Eventually, this can cause them to question their self-worth and self-esteem. This state will further aggravate the difficulties they were having in the first place — a vicious circle.

Others may arrive at school already having self-image challenges for some other reason. These can be detected through school performance, and measures to correct the situation can be taken.

PAT techniques can help these children rebuild their self-esteem by developing confidence and belief in themselves.

Peer pressure

Peer pressure is a situation which begins to affect children early as they interact and desire to fit into the school peer society. It reaches its peak in high school and abruptly ceases at graduation when the temporary society is dissolved. Peer pressure is mentioned here because it is chiefly a school-related phenomenon, but the real effects are experienced at home by the parents as their children begin to reject their parents' desires in favor of the demands of the peer group.

It is our belief, however, that the influence of peer groups lessens when young adults are raised to view themselves as worthy, creative, independent beings. They know how to resist demands which confuse their identity. Learning to visualize themselves as leaders and believing in themselves strengthen their ability to handle this situation.

Getting along with others

In school, children are exposed to many different students. As they move up in grades, not only must they deal with their own classmates, but they interact with children and young adults in higher and lower grades. This situation can present challenges in interpersonal relationships.

Individuals need to learn to get along with others if they expect to be successful in life. Teachers should be on the alert for problems in this area because detecting them is as important, if not more so, than many other situations arising in school. If a student forgets all of his algebra, he can still be successful in mature life. (I do not mean to belittle algebra. Personally, I always enjoyed and still do the mental stimulation of the subject!) But, if a student fails to get along with others, his whole future as a happy adult will be jeopardized. Teachers can detect these problems and bring them to the attention of the parents or student, if old enough to appreciate its significance. Teachers who initiate attempts to teach students to resolve these difficulties might find these to be the most significant accomplishments of their teaching careers.

Early vs. late onset of school

In Chapter 7 I promised to return to the subject of the value of kindergarten and early school.

My main objection to kindergarten is that although it is schooling, it has too much of a play environment. When young children first attend school they should know it is school and it is serious business. Once that point of *mental discipline* is made, the child will psychologically disassociate school from the play world — an important goal to achieve. The kindergarten experience accomplishes very little, if any, meaningful learning experience. Children would benefit more from *Sesame Street*.

Many 6-year olds are not even psychologically mature enough to enter the first grade. Some educators and psychologists believe that early schooling can do a child more damage than good and believe that 8 years of age is a better time to start school. Earlier than this the child's brain, vision, hearing, perception, emotions, and physical growth are not suitably mature. Formal training, insisting that a child read, write, spell, and do math before his brain is capable of such tasks can result in an overload of his nervous system. In time some of these children become frustrated and discouraged by their failure. Many are turned off by school by the time they reach the third or fourth grade and suffer lifelong learning problems. In addition, some believe that a child's value system should be truly established at home before he is exposed to the influence of strangers and other children.

To say that all children should wait till they are eight would deprive those who mature earlier from moving along with their formal education. For years it has been generally accepted that 6 or 7 years of age is a reasonable time to start school. It would appear reasonable to have a sliding age scale between 6 to 8 so that 6-year olds who are mature enough could begin and those who are not could wait till 7 or 8. One or two years difference in chronological age has less significance than one or two years difference in psychological maturity. We may well avert many learning disabilities by considering the overall maturity of children entering school. Well, anyway, it is something to consider.

The application of **non-competitive** mental training techniques described in Chapter 5 would hasten a child's development and not threaten him because the child would create his own images compatible with his level of maturity.

Summary

Schools are charged with the responsibility of educating children and training them to think and use their minds for self-development. Discipline is required in the classroom to establish order in the classroom. Although learning is serious business, it can be a fun and games experience to be enjoyed by the student and teacher.

Learning disabilities, such as poor concentration, poor memory, dyslexia and hyperactivity, can be annoying and frustrating for all concerned: children, parents, and teachers. A combination of a good natural diet devoid of chemical additives and application of PAT techniques would significantly help all those experiencing difficulties in learning.

Teachers could help students deal also with problems of deteriorating self-esteem, peer pressure, getting along with others. Mental and psychological maturity are probably better criteria than chronological age for determining time of onset of school.

The garden advisers

Frequently the gardener and helpers are confronted with situations requiring the expert opinion of horticulturists from the Extension Service. Sometimes the work in the garden becomes too much for the gardener to do alone and it is then necessary to bring in some contract labor. Although the experts advise and the contract labor helps, it still is the responsibility of the gardener to implement the recommendations.

So it is in the garden of life. As children grow, parents ask teachers, counsellors, ministers, and others to advise and help in the work of raising the children. Parents, teachers and other helpers should never lose sight of the fact that, although responsibilities for the child's upbringing are shared, it still is the main responsibilitiy of parents to provide the child's early learning experiences.

CHAPTER 15

THE CHALLENGE OF RAISING CHILDREN TO HAVE POSITIVE ATTITUDES

Introduction

The challenge of raising children is not with insuring that they grow and develop normal physically. Although there are still a few segments of our society today having to concern themselves about this, generally, adequate health facilities **are** available to provide top-notch medical care even to the indigent.

The challenge of raising children is not in providing items necessary to subsist, such as food, running water and a toilet, nor in providing modern *creature comforts* such as radio, TV, and automobile. These items are all readily available to most of the population with the exception of only a very few.

Challenge is not in providing education to the masses of children reaching school age each year, even though it is sad to observe that with the amount of tax money used to establish the most elaborate school system the world has ever known, many young adults are graduating from high school **unable** to read and write.

I acknowledge that challenges do exist in **completing** the above-mentioned tasks and possibly there are reasons why it may never be done. The inability to complete these tasks may depend upon the attitude of each individual.

How can individuals get anything positive out of life if they believe that life is a "bummer" and not worth living? How can children learn in school when they think that "school stinks"? How can individuals succeed in their jobs when they are nervous, uptight, negative and they feel the whole world is crumbling down upon them? How can parents raise their children to have a positive attitude about life when they constantly affirm that the "world isn't what it used to be" and "it's a bad time to bring up children."

The real challenge in life would appear to be for individuals to **learn** to develop positive attitudes which would allow them to be receptive, to experience health, success, wealth, prosperity, and, of course, enlightenment, rather than to create negative attitudes which are self-defeating and self-destructive. The word "learn" was underscored for a purpose. The challenge is not to teach positive attitudes. Many individuals are doing this today. Success in developing positive attitudes depends upon the receptiveness of the learner and the patience and understanding of the teacher. Louis Pasteur said, "Chance favors the mind which is prepared." So it is with many things. Individuals will experience in direct proportion to their receptiveness and belief. Although a dynamic positive teacher may be a strong convincing influence, it is still the responsibility of each individual to do it for himself. If you are not yet convinced after having

THE CHALLENGE OF RAISING CHILDREN 217

read this book, **you** have failed to read it with an open mind.

But, **you** tell me, how can we learn to develop and maintain positive attitudes about life when we are bombarded from almost every source today with so much negativity and hopelessness: TV, radio, newspapers, movies, relatives, friends, politicians, etc.? I must believe that it can be developed. I **do** believe. **We** must believe together, and, as we do, more will.

The purpose of this chapter is to present a philosophy of learning how to develop and maintain positive and creative attitudes about oneself, others, the world around him, and life in general. In the author's opinion, believing in this philosophy and practicing it will cause one to experience it. This chapter also will present an overview of what was presented in the previous chapters.

The philosophy

We are endowed with body, mind, and spirit. The spirit which **is** life is expressed, while we are alive, through our mind and body: the mind for mental and emotional expression, the body for physical expression. To function as a whole person, body, mind and spirit must be unified and act as one, that is, to be *holy* or *whole in one*.

Our mind is a most unique creation because **it** can create from energy. This is the essence of creation. Einstein's theory of relativity, expressed in the well-known formula, $E=mc^2$, essentially states that there is a **reversible** relationship between energy (E) and physical mass (m): that, when mass is activated to the speed of light squared (c^2), it is transformed into energy. We have accomplished this with the atomic bomb and nuclear power. This transformation of mass into energy is what happens in death and it is the most commonly occurring event in nature and in the whole Universe.

The equation being reversible, the reaction also goes the other way: energy can be transformed into matter when it is slowed down to the degree equivalent to the speed of light squared. This is the act of creation, which is also continuously occurring in the Universe as evidenced by the creation of new planets.

Although the average human mind has not achieved that degree of development, sophistication and **evolvement** to be able to create matter by sheer mental energy instantaneously, it can create in other ways.

First, the mind has the ability to create ideas by transforming mental energy into organized thought forms. These thought forms are real and can be conveyed by expression through the physical body.

Second, these thoughts can be conveyed as discrete energy entities to the minds of other individuals *(telepathy)*. Thoughts can enter our minds from the mind of others and elsewhere *(ESP and clairvoyance)*, or be directed into objects where the energy can either move or alter the physical appearance or state of the object *(psychokinesis)*.

Third, these thoughts and ideas all get stored within our subconscious mental biocomputer from which they can be retrieved at will *(memory)*.

Fourth, our thoughts form the basis of our *habits*, which are convenient automatic packages of discrete programmings. Habits also stored within the subconscious are ways by which the subconscious mind (high-energy state) can carry out functions without requiring input, from the conscious mind (low-energy state).

Fifth, our *behavior* represents habits activated into action. Whether behavior is positive or negative depends upon whether the programmed habits are positive or negative.

Sixth, our conscious mind creates the initial thought, which gets stored and eventually transformed into a subconscious habit. Therefore, it becomes a *conscious responsibility* of the individual to decide whether his initial thoughts and ideas are positive, thereby making his habits positive programmed entities, resulting in his acting and experiencing positive events.

Seventh, our inner subconscious mind develops and maintains the important and meaningful beliefs about ourselves (self-abilities, self-worth, self-esteem) and about what we can do. **Belief creates reality**. Whatever we truly believe at our inner subconscious level is what we are going to create and experience in our lives. Therefore, since only **we** have power over our thoughts and beliefs, only **we** are responsible for what we experience.

Eighth, our belief depends upon our attitudes. We will be positive in our belief if our attitudes are positive; negative beliefs result from negative attitudes.

Ninth, our attitudes are also habit-programmed entities, many of which are initially created by our conscious mind and stored as such. Others are subconscious creations resulting from information already stored in the subconscious.

Tenth, we have the power to create our attitudes. We can train ourselves to be positive through a system of Positive Attitude Training (PAT), so that we can develop a positive, uplifting, and creative belief system, rather than to allow ourselves to absorb the negativity of the *negative* *creative imaginings* of others. We can affect our whole destiny by our thinking.

Application of philosophy

The application of this philosophy is essentially the subject matter of this book. Throughout this book the theme has been that we experience in direct proportion to our beliefs. If you wish your life to be a positive uplifting creative experience, you must first believe that you can do it, and then do it. Developing and maintaining positive attitudes will not only cause you to be receptive but also cause you to experience the positive events you desire.

Our attitudes are deep-seated habits stored within our subconscious mind which functions at a high-energy state. Since changing bad habits to positive ones takes so much effort and energy, it would be ideal to prevent bad habits and develop positive ones in childhood.

Chapter 1 discussed the importance of teaching children how to be positive through Positive Attitude Training (PAT) which is defined as a system by which the individual learns how to develop a positive, constructive uplifting and creative attitude toward **all** phases of life's experiences. It is primarily the parents' responsibility to institute this training and to insure its continued reinforcement until young adults are mature enough to continue the process themselves.

Chapter 2 describes some aspects of child development as these relate to his relationship with himself first, then others. The significance of self-awareness is introduced to aid the child in getting to know himself — an important goal to achieve before he can know and truly appreciate those around him with whom he must interact all his life. The child will need to deal with his parents and other authority figures, such as teachers, as he develops increasing authority over himself and before he accepts the role of supervising others. He must learn to deal with friends and peers.

PAT instituted in the home as a group effort can help not only the children but also the whole team to accept themselves as independent creative spirits and others as fellow travelers who must share the trip of life. PAT can help children develop the awareness *(self-awareness)* that they are independent spirits with almost infinite creative potential. This process well equips them to achieve their innermost goals and wildest dreams.

Chapter 3 deals with the importance of developing and maintaining throughout life a strong belief that God is here **now** and desires to assist us in our journey. We need but ask. Since we share in His Divinity a continuous contact is required for optimum spiritual health.

Chapter 4 describes how the mind functions and suggests mental exercises which are the keys to PAT. Since the mind functions like a highly sophisticated biocomputer, what comes out reflects what goes in. What goes into the minds of children will be reflected in their attitudes and behavior throughout their lives as adults.

Children can learn how to train their subconscious mind so that being positive becomes automatic behavior. An important aspect of this training is to learn to apply the four keys to self-development and self-realization (i.e., self-responsibility, self-awareness, self-control, and self-discipline), which are important elements in communicating desires to the subconscious.

Positive Attitude Training (PAT) techniques are

described in Chapter 5. Through mental games children can be taught *affirmation*, one of the key ways of convincing the subconscious that you mean business and of developing a positive belief factor; *meditation*, whereby you can tap your inner mental powers to transform desires into reality; and *guided imagery*, the process of creating and visualizing with your imagination situations as you want them to be.

Chapters 6, 7, and 8 deal with particular challenges facing children in three of their major environments, namely the home, school, and play, respectively. These chapters are not meant to be a compendium of details influencing the psychosocial development of children. Rather, they deal with some important factors parents and teachers need to consider as they teach children how to grow and develop.

Since the functioning of the mind and, subsequently, the behavior of children are affected by prescription medicines and drugs, Chapter 9 evolved. Drugs (both illegal and legitimate) can seriously affect the ability of children and young adults to develop positive attitudes about life and the body's mechanisms to handle some physical dis-ease states.

The food we eat also affects mental functions, especially in children (Chapter 10). Certain toxic foods and chemical food additives interfere with the ability of many children to concentrate and pay attention, resulting in impairment of learning and memory. Attention to diet and employing PAT are prime considerations in solving learning and behavior challenges in childhood.

A reasonable amount of good aerobic physical activity or exercise increases blood flow to the tissues and actually rejuvenates the cells and it increases mental acuity (Chapter 11). You begin to think more clearly, your emotions improve and the spirit within comes alive.

Chapter 12 discusses the importance and methods of spiritual training in the overall development of children.

Since children depend upon parents and teachers to help them develop their minds as useful entities, the responsibilities of parents (Chapter 13) and of teachers and the school system (Chapter 14) were discussed. These chapters may appear to be tough on both parents and teachers. They are meant to be. The adult will not have an opportunity to go through his childhood learning experiences again. So it must be done correctly or nearly so the first time. Our viewpoint may not provide **all** the answers, but they do provide a better alternative to what the average child is exposed to today.

The child who grows up negatively with a poor self-image, unable to handle the normal challenges of life, has only to thank the adults around him for this legacy.

Conclusion

Let us consider who and what children really are. They are who we were. They are what the world will be.

Let us do for them what we would have liked others to have done for us: prepare us to be what we could have been.

This is what *awakening the genius* though PAT is all about.

The garden at harvest

The garden scenario is complete and harvest time is at hand. At first glance, this may seem to be the end of the picture, but it is only the beginning. Crops are harvested for food. Seeds are harvested and stored to be used in the spring when the process begins again. Life in the garden is a continuous on-going process of planting, growth, development, fruition, and planting again.

The garden of life is no different. Parents plant the seed that brings forth the child. The child grows, matures, is harvested and plants again. How a child grows depends on the care, commitment and concern of parents, teachers and others and the interaction with peers. Essential to a fruitful life is the early realization of the genius within each child, and the drawing out of this genius by providing proper and positive thoughts and attitudes, good food and exercises, spiritual disciplines, and the reverence for all of life.

SUGGESTED READINGS
and references referred to in this book

Sugar Blues, by William Dufty, Warner Books, Inc., New York, 1975.

Why Your Child Is Hyperactive, by Ben F. Feingold, Random House, New York, 1975.

The Kirlian Aura: Photographing the Galaxies of Life, Stanley Krippner and Daniel Rubin, Editors, Doubleday & Company, Inc., Anchor Books edition, Garden City, New York, 1974.

Suggestology and Outlines of Suggestopedy, by Georgi Lazanov, Gordon and Breach, Park Ave., New York, NY 10016, 1978.

Superlearning, by Sheila Ostrander and Lynn Schroeder with Nancy Ostrander, Delacorte Press/Confucian Press, New York, 1979.

The Power of Positive Thinking, by Norman Vincent Peale, Prentice-Hall, Inc., 1956.

How To Benefit From Stress, by Nicola M. Tauraso and L. Richard Batzler, Hidden Valley Press, Frederick, Maryland, 1979.

Manual of Positive Attitude Training Techniques for Children and Young Adults, Nicola M. Tauraso and L. Richard Batzler, Hidden Valley Press, Frederick, Maryland, 1981.

Dietary Goals for the United States, by the Select Committee on Nutrition and Human Needs of the United States Senate, U.S. Government Printing Office, 1975.

Child Guidance, by Ellen G. White, Southern Publishing Association, Nashville, Tennessee, 1954.

OTHER BOOKS BY THE AUTHORS
(How To Obtain Them)

How To Benefit From Stress by Nicola M. Tauraso and L. Richard Batzler, 1979, Hidden Valley Press, $10.95.

Manual of Positive Attitude Training Techniques for Children and Young Adults by Nicola M. Tauraso and L. Richard Batzler, 1981, Hidden Valley Press, $15.00 (Manual contains 2 cassette tapes).

Recommendations for Healthful Living – An Holistic Approach, a health program of The GOTACH Center For Health, 1981, Hidden Valley Press, $5.95.

These books can be purchased by sending the appropriate fee to Hidden Valley Press, 7051 Poole Jones Road, Frederick, Maryland 21701.

All proceeds (royalties) derived from the sale of these publications are donated to The GOTACH Center For Health for building a residential/camp facility dedicated to and to be used by children, to teach and help them "awaken" their "genius," and for use by children and adults who desire to explore creative alternatives of healing.